Better Homes & Gardens

QUICK
HOMEMADE

FAST, FRESH MEALS IN 30 MINUTES

HOUGHTON MIFFLIN HARCOURT
BOSTON · NEW YORK · 2019

BETTER HOMES & GARDENS® QUICK HOMEMADE

Editor: Jessica Christensen
Contributing Project Manager: Shelli McConnell, Purple Pear Publishing, Inc.
Contributing Copy Editor: Terri Fredrickson
Contributing Proofreader: Gretchen Kauffman
Test Kitchen Director: Lynn Blanchard
Test Kitchen Product Supervisor: Colleen Weeden
Test Kitchen Culinary Professionals: Sarah Brekke; Linda Brewer, RD; Heidi Engelhardt; Juli Hale; Paige Havey; Sammy Mila
Contributing Photographers: Jason Donnelly, Andy Lyons, Blaine Moats, Brie Passano
Contributing Stylists: Kelsey Bulat, Greg Luna, Charlie Worthington
Administrative Assistant: Courtney Bush

BETTER HOMES & GARDENS® MAGAZINE

Editor in Chief: Stephen Orr
Creative Director: Jennifer D. Madara
Executive Food Editor: Jan Miller
Design Director: Stephanie Hunter

HOUGHTON MIFFLIN HARCOURT

Executive Editor: Anne Ficklen
Managing Editor: Marina Padakis Lowry
Art Director: Tai Blanche
Production Director: Tom Hyland

WATERBURY PUBLICATIONS, INC.

Design Director: Ken Carlson
Editorial Director: Lisa Kingsley
Associate Editorial Director: Tricia Bergman
Associate Design Director: Doug Samuelson
Production Assistant: Mindy Samuelson

Pictured on front cover:
Bagel and Lox Skillet Strata, recipe, *page 32*

hmhbooks.com

Library of Congress Cataloging-in-Publication Data is available.

ISBN 978-1-328-62437-6 (pbk)
Book design by Waterbury Publications, Inc., Des Moines, Iowa.

Printed in China.

SCP 10 9 8 7 6 5 4 3 2 1

INTRODUCTION

The work week is busy—we'll help you simplify your mealtime strategy so you can get fresh and delicious food on the table fast. Each recipe in this book uses minimally processed ingredients and only takes 30 minutes or less from start to finish. Choose from on-trend recipes with flavors your family craves—noodle bowls, skillet meals, sheet-pan suppers, sandwiches, salads, breakfasts, and more. Start with "Step Up Your Prep," *page 6,* to get you and your kitchen ready for streamlined dinner solutions. Look for these other useful icons as you flip through the pages.

We included tags throughout this cookbook, which are located underneath some recipe titles:

INSTANT MEAL	HEALTHY	SUPER QUICK

INSTANT MEAL Uses a multifunction electric or stove-top pressure cooker. These recipes can be prepped and cooked in under 30 minutes. However, times for bringing the cooker to pressure and releasing pressure will vary by cooker and are not included in calculating times.

HEALTHY Meets criteria for lower calories and fat for healthful eating

SUPER QUICK Recipes can be made in 20 minutes or less

Tips with some recipes indicate the following:

[SPEED IT UP]

Accelerate the prep of a recipe with a simple strategy or preprepped ingredient.

[MAKE A SWAP]

Trade a recipe ingredient that may use up something from your pantry or better suit your taste.

[FINISH WITH FLAVOR]

Bump up the flavor of a dish right before serving with a squeeze of this or a sprinkle of that.

Potato Chip Baked
Chicken Fingers, *page 138*

CONTENTS

STEP UP YOUR PREP

Organization and planning are key to preparing meals quickly. Get the right equipment and organize your kitchen and pantry for efficient cooking. Then shop with specific meals in mind so you have what you need when you are ready to cook.

GET THE RIGHT GEAR

You may have a fully stocked kitchen, but these tools are what you'll use most for quick cooking.

Pots and Pans Use the right size. Food cooks faster when it has enough room. The recipes in this book give specific pan sizes for best results.

Skillets These are quick-cooking workhorses. Have a couple of sizes (large = 10-inch, extra-large = 12-inch). Select skillets that can be used on the stove top as well as in the oven. These are all-metal pans—including the handle. When in doubt, check with the manufacturer.

Knives A paring knife, chef's knife, and maybe a serrated knife are really all you need. Keep them SHARP so chopping and slicing go faster.

Kitchen Scissors These make short work of chopping fresh herbs and are handy for snipping bits of fat off chicken pieces and cutting up bacon strips.

Gadgets These gadgets are real time-savers in the kitchen: apple corer/slicer, flexible cutting boards, mini food processor, garlic press, rasp-style graters, immersion blender, and a good-quality vegetable peeler.

The Ultimate Gadget Your smart phone can be the best kitchen assistant. Use it to look up recipes, make grocery lists, place grocery orders, play how-to videos, monitor cooking time, take pictures, research ingredients, find ingredient substitutions, and more. Use a search engine to do these tasks or download specific apps to streamline your time in the kitchen.

UNDER PRESSURE

Pressure cookers cook food fast. There are two main types of pressure cookers: electric and stove-top. You can also find electric multifunction cookers, such as an Instant Pot.

ELECTRIC

These models look like slow cookers (and often have multiple functions that include slow cooking). They are easy to set and require no further supervision.

Brown and Sauté Most models have a sauté function that lets you brown meat and sauté veggies without using another pan. Cook in batches to prevent overcrowding, which steams rather than caramelizes.

Everything In! Once the meat is browned, add other ingredients as directed. Lock the lid and adjust the pressure valve to closed position. Select setting and time. The digital display will indicate when the cooker has gotten to pressure (usually about 15 minutes) and the actual cooking time starts to count down.

Let off Steam When cooking time is done, the cooker will begin to depressurize, which is called "natural release." This takes about 15 minutes. When pressure has dropped, the indicator will sink and the lid will unlock. If the lid is still locked after 15 minutes or you want to "quick release," you can carefully open the pressure valve using long-handled tongs to let out any remaining steam. Follow recipe instructions for natural or quick release to ensure proper doneness.

Open Sesame! The food inside is still extremely hot, so when opening the lid, lift the side away from you first.

STOVE-TOP

This cooker looks like a large saucepan with a lid that locks tight. It is heated on the stove and requires that you monitor the pressure regulator during the cooking process. You can brown meat in this cooker before pressure cooking.

Use It Right After locking the lid, set the pressure

valve per the user's manual. Bring it to pressure over medium-high heat (you'll know it's there when steam comes out of the valve). Reduce heat to maintain steady pressure (this keeps the pressure indicator up) for the full cooking time. Remove from stove; let pressure come down naturally (watch for pressure indicator to drop).

PLAN FOR QUICKER COOKING

1. Take a meal-prep moment. Mentally walk through the parts of your meal (i.e., main, sides, salad). Organize tasks so you start with those that take the most time and decide where you can bundle steps.

2. Heat them up. Two things that take a long time and can catch you unprepared are preheating the oven and boiling water. Get that oven turned on and start heating a pot of water before you do anything else. To get water to boil faster, cover it with a lid. (BTW, always start with cold water since it comes right from the tap. Hot water routes through your water heater and possibly a water softener first and may contain more impurities.)

3. Pull your pans. Get out all the pans and equipment you'll need for the meal. This saves time digging through cupboards on the fly, especially after you've started cooking and have messy hands.

4. Gather the goods. Open the fridge and pantry once and set everything you'll need on the counter. Divide the ingredients by recipe and the order you need to cook them. This visual outline helps keep you efficient.

5. Bundle your prep. Wash and cut up all vegetables for the main dish, side dish, and/or salad. Separate them into bowls. Then prepare any meat. Start cooking the items that take the longest first.

6. Meanwhile ... Many recipes will start a step with the word "meanwhile," meaning you can work on a second part of the recipe while the first part cooks or stands—while pasta cooks, make the sauce. You can apply this multitasking to your whole meal—while a sheet-pan dinner bakes, make a salad.

10 HACKS FOR FASTER MEAL PREP

1 Plan the week's meals on the weekend (or any designated day of the week). Go shopping and buy all the ingredients you need and prep some things in advance. For example, chop veggies for a stir-fry or salads and put them in a resealable plastic bag.

2 Give frozen meats enough time to thaw in the refrigerator rather than on the counter, which encourages bacterial growth.

3 Cook extra meat to use in another meal. Toss a few extra chicken breasts on the grill to use in a pasta salad or chicken tacos the next day.

4 If you need roasted chicken for one meal, buy an entire rotisserie chicken. Shred the extra, package it in resealable plastic bags, and freeze so it's ready to grab when you want it.

5 Cut chicken breasts in half horizontally so you have thinner cuts that cook faster.

6 If a recipe calls for crisp-cooked and crumbled bacon, chop up bacon before cooking—smaller bits cook faster. Or shave off even more time by buying precooked real bacon pieces or strips.

7 Select cut-up fresh veggies, like cauliflower or broccoli florets, in the produce section and save on that prep step. Raid the salad bar to get just-right amounts.

8 Snag packaged specialty veggies like riced cauliflower and broccoli or noodled zucchini and sweet potatoes from the produce and freezer sections.

9 Don't bother peeling all fresh produce. Give carrots, beets, and potatoes a good scrub and eat the skins, which are loaded with fiber and nutrients.

10 Use healthful convenience foods like canned beans, diced tomatoes, cooked rice in bags, and fresh pasta. Peeled hard-boiled eggs are readily available, too.

LINE PANS WITH FOIL BEFORE BAKING OR BROILING. FOR QUICK CLEANUP, JUST GATHER THE EDGES AND BALL UP THE FOIL.

KEEP A GARBAGE BOWL PUT ANY TRIMMINGS AND TRASH IN ONE PLACE. DUMP IT ONCE WHEN YOU'RE DONE WITH DINNER.

DO A FRIDGE INVENTORY (PANTRY, TOO!)

There's an app for that. Knowing what you have on hand makes it easier to plan meals and avoid waste. Find a smart phone app to help you quickly track what you have on hand when making your shopping list.

Clean out the fridge and pantry. Get rid of outdated foods. Organize shelves in categories that make sense to you. You'll save time if you know right where to find items.

See-through containers make it easy to quickly ID things. Buy stackable square containers rather than round ones since they don't waste space.

KEEP THE SIDES SIMPLE

Use one of our recipes for the main dish, then add a simple side dish or salad to round out the meal.

- Steam green beans and toss with sautéed onions and crisp-cooked bacon.
- Pan-roast Brussels sprouts and toss with orange marmalade and a splash of cider vinegar.
- Steam snow peas and carrots and toss with a bottled Asian sauce.
- Pan-sauté red peppers and onions, then toss them with a purchased cooked whole grain blend.
- Drizzle sliced tomatoes with balsamic vinegar, then sprinkle with fresh basil, salt, and pepper.
- Top a lettuce wedge with a vinaigrette, toasted almonds, feta, and dried cherries.
- Slice pears and top with crumbled blue cheese.
- Toss fresh spinach with apples, red onions, and poppy seed dressing.

CLEAN AS YOU GO A BIG CLEANUP SESSION AT THE END OF A MEAL IS NO FUN. IF YOU WASH UP AS YOU GO AND KEEP YOUR WORK SURFACES CLEAN, IT KEEPS THE TASK MANAGEABLE.

BREAKFAST

IT'S EASY TO RISE AND SHINE WHEN BREAKFAST TASTES THIS GOOD. OR BETTER YET, FLIP THE DAY AROUND AND WHIP UP A BREAKFAST-FOR-DINNER OF OMELETS, FRITTATAS, PIZZAS, SANDWICHES, OR BURRITOS.

CAST-IRON BAKED EGGS AND HAM

SUPER QUICK	MAKES 4 SERVINGS

1 Tbsp. butter

½ cup chopped cooked ham

¼ cup sliced leek or green onions

6 eggs

½ cup heavy cream or half-and-half

¼ cup shredded Gruyère or sharp white cheddar cheese (1 oz.)

2 Tbsp. chopped fresh basil or Italian parsley

Salt and black pepper

Sourdough or multigrain bread, toasted

1. Preheat oven to 400°F. Melt butter in a 9- or 10-inch cast-iron skillet over medium. Add ham and leek; cook and stir 2 to 3 minutes or until leek is soft.

2. Break an egg into a custard cup. Slip egg into skillet. Repeat with remaining eggs, evenly spacing yolks. Drizzle cream around eggs. Sprinkle with cheese and basil. Bake 5 to 7 minutes or until egg whites are set and yolks are thickened. Season with salt and pepper. Serve with toast.

EACH SERVING 378 cal., 26 g fat (13 g sat. fat), 340 mg chol., 693 mg sodium, 17 g carb., 1 g fiber, 2 g sugars, 19 g pro.

OPEN-FACE BREAKFAST MONTE CRISTOS

SUPER QUICK	MAKES 4 SERVINGS

6   eggs

⅓   cup fat-free milk

4   slices firm-texture sourdough rye or whole grain bread

3   tsp. coconut oil or butter

4   slices Canadian-style bacon

2   Tbsp. fig jam

4   slices reduced-fat Swiss cheese

4   fresh basil leaves, thinly sliced

    Salt and black pepper

1. In a shallow bowl whisk together two of the eggs and the milk. Dip bread slices into egg mixture, dipping 10 seconds per side. In an extra-large skillet melt 2 tsp. of the oil over medium. Add dipped bread; cook 4 to 6 minutes or until golden, turning once. Remove from skillet and keep warm.

2. In same skillet melt the remaining 1 tsp. oil over medium. Break remaining four eggs into skillet; reduce heat to low. Cook 3 to 4 minutes or until whites are set and yolks start to thicken, adding Canadian bacon the last 2 minutes, turning bacon once. For fried eggs over-easy, turn eggs and cook 30 seconds more.

3. Spread bread slices with jam; top with cheese, Canadian bacon, and fried eggs. Sprinkle with basil and season to taste with salt and pepper.

EACH SERVING 332 cal., 16 g fat (8 g sat. fat), 305 mg chol., 679 mg sodium, 23 g carb., 1 g fiber, 9 g sugars, 22 g pro.

[MAKE A SWAP]

USE BOLD FLAVORS IN THESE SANDWICHES. IF YOU DON'T HAVE FIG JAM, YOU CAN SPREAD BREAD SLICES WITH ORANGE MARMALADE OR JALAPEÑO JELLY.

EASY OMELETS

SUPER QUICK	MAKES 2 SERVINGS

4 eggs
¼ cup water
1 Tbsp. butter
½ cup chopped tomato
¼ cup sliced sautéed mushrooms
¼ cup chopped cooked broccoli
¼ cup sliced cooked asparagus
2 Tbsp. shredded cheddar cheese (optional)
Sliced avocado (optional)
Cracked black pepper (optional)

1. In a medium bowl whisk together eggs and the water until combined but not frothy.

2. In a medium nonstick skillet melt half of the butter over medium-high just until a drop of water sizzles. (Or coat skillet with nonstick cooking spray.) Add half of the egg mixture (about ½ cup). It should start to set immediately.

3. Using an inverted spatula, push cooked portions at edges toward center so uncooked portions flow underneath, tilting pan as needed.

4. When top is just set, spread about half each of the tomato, mushrooms, broccoli, asparagus, and, if desired, cheese over half of the omelet. Using spatula, fold omelet in half over filling. Invert onto a plate. Repeat with remaining butter, egg mixture, and filling. If desired, top omelets with avocado and/or pepper.

EACH SERVING 212 cal., 15 g fat (7 g sat. fat), 387 mg chol., 195 mg sodium, 4 g carb., 1 g fiber, 2 g sugars, 14 g pro.

Greek Omelet Prepare as directed, except use ¼ cup each chopped fresh spinach and canned artichoke hearts, 2 Tbsp. crumbled feta cheese, and 1 Tbsp. chopped pitted Kalamata olives for the filling.
EACH SERVING 239 cal., 19 g fat (8 g sat. fat), 396 mg chol., 484 mg sodium, 3 g carb., 1 g fiber, 1 g sugars, 14 g pro.

Italian Omelet Prepare as directed, except use ¼ cup each chopped fresh basil and cut-up roasted red sweet pepper, 1 link chopped Italian-flavor cooked chicken sausage, and 1 Tbsp. grated Parmesan cheese for the filling.
EACH SERVING 278 cal., 19 g fat (8 g sat. fat), 3 g carb., 422 mg chol., 551 mg sodium, 0 g fiber, 1 g sugars, 21 g pro.

PROSCIUTTO AND EGG BREAKFAST SALAD

HEALTHY	MAKES 4 SERVINGS

1 lemon

½ cup packed fresh Italian parsley leaves

½ cup packed fresh basil leaves or dill

1 clove garlic, halved

1 small avocado, halved, seeded, and peeled

3 Tbsp. plain low-fat yogurt

2 Tbsp. olive oil

2 Tbsp. water

Salt and freshly ground black pepper

1 large carrot, peeled

2 heads butterhead (Bibb or Boston) lettuce, torn into bite-size pieces (11 cups)

1¾ cups thinly sliced radishes

3 thin slices prosciutto

4 cups water

1 tsp. white vinegar

4 eggs

1. For dressing, remove ½ tsp. zest and squeeze 2 Tbsp. juice from lemon. In a food processor combine parsley, basil, and garlic; cover and pulse until finely chopped. Add lemon zest and juice, one of the avocado halves, the yogurt, oil, and the 2 Tbsp. water. Cover and process until smooth. Season to taste with salt and pepper.

2. Chop remaining avocado half. Using a vegetable peeler, cut carrot lengthwise into thin ribbons. In a large bowl combine lettuce, radishes, chopped avocado, and carrot ribbons.

3. In a large skillet cook prosciutto over medium just until browned and crisp. Remove from skillet; cut into strips or crumble into bite-size pieces.

4. In the same skillet bring the 4 cups water and the vinegar to boiling; reduce heat to simmering. Break eggs, one at a time, into a cup; slip eggs into simmering water. Simmer 3 to 5 minutes or until whites are completely set and yolks start to thicken. Remove eggs with a slotted spoon.

5. Drizzle lettuce mixture with dressing; toss to coat. Top servings with prosciutto and eggs.

EACH SERVING 247 cal., 18 g fat (4 g sat. fat), 189 mg chol., 419 mg sodium, 11 g carb., 5 g fiber, 4 g sugars, 12 g pro.

[SPEED IT UP]

LOOK FOR AN AVOCADO-BASED SALAD DRESSING OR EVEN CREAMY CAESAR TO USE INSTEAD OF MAKING YOUR OWN IN STEP 1.

AVOCADO EGG BAKES

MAKES 2 SERVINGS

Nonstick cooking spray
2 thin slices deli ham
1 avocado, halved and seeded
2 eggs
½ tsp. everything bagel seasoning*

1. Preheat oven to 425°F. Coat a 9×5-inch loaf pan with cooking spray. Pat ham slices with paper towel to dry.

2. Scoop out enough of the flesh of each avocado half to leave a ½-inch shell.** Place a slice of ham in each half and gently press to secure to avocado. Place halves in the prepared pan. Crack an egg into each avocado cup. Loosely cover pan with foil.

3. Bake about 15 minutes or until egg white is set and yolk is desired consistency. Sprinkle eggs with seasoning.

*Tip If you can't find bagel seasoning at your supermarket, make your own. In a bowl stir together 1 tsp. each sesame seeds and poppy seeds, ½ tsp each dried minced onion and dried minced garlic, and ¼ tsp. each kosher salt and dried lemon peel.

**Tip Mash the scooped-out avocado flesh with some lemon or lime juice, salt, and black pepper for a quick guacamole.

EACH SERVING 206 cal., 16 g fat (3 g sat. fat), 194 mg chol., 273 mg sodium, 7 g carb., 5 g fiber, 1 g sugars, 11 g pro.

CALIFORNIA BREAKFAST BURRITOS

MAKES 6 SERVINGS

4 eggs
¼ cup milk
¼ tsp. salt
   Dash black pepper
1 Tbsp. olive oil
4 slices turkey bacon, crisp-cooked and crumbled
⅓ cup sliced or chopped pitted ripe olives
6 8-inch whole wheat flour tortillas or flour tortillas
½ of a ripe avocado, seeded, peeled, and thinly sliced
⅓ cup finely chopped tomato
½ cup shredded Monterey Jack cheese (2 oz.)

1. In a small bowl whisk together eggs, milk, salt, and pepper. In a large skillet heat oil over medium; pour in egg mixture. Cook, without stirring, until mixture begins to set on the bottom and around edge. Using a spatula or large spoon, lift and fold the partially cooked egg mixture so the uncooked portion flows underneath. Stir in bacon and olives. Continue cooking 2 to 3 minutes more or until egg mixture is cooked through but is still glossy and moist. Remove from heat.

2. Meanwhile, heat tortillas according to package directions. Divide egg mixture among tortillas, spooning it horizontally across the centers of the tortillas. Top with avocado and tomato. Sprinkle with cheese. Fold bottom edges of tortillas up and over filling, fold in opposite sites, and roll up tortillas. Serve immediately.

EACH SERVING 295 cal., 16 g fat (5 g sat. fat), 140 mg chol., 704 mg sodium, 25 g carb., 4 g fiber, 3 g sugars, 13 g pro.

Veggie Breakfast Burritos Omit turkey bacon, olives, avocado, and tomato. Substitute provolone cheese for the Monterey Jack cheese. In a large skillet heat 1 Tbsp. olive oil over medium-high. Add 1 cup frozen hash brown potatoes; 6 asparagus spears, trimmed and cut into 1-inch pieces; ¾ cup coarsely chopped zucchini; and ½ cup chopped red sweet pepper. Cook and stir 8 to 10 minutes or until potatoes are tender and beginning to brown. Remove from skillet. Wipe out skillet. In the same skillet prepare eggs as directed. Divide vegetable mixture among the tortillas. Top with egg mixture. Sprinkle with cheese. Continue as directed.
EACH SERVING 309 cal., 14 g fat (6 g sat. fat), 140 mg chol., 572 mg sodium, 31 g carb., 4 g fiber, 4 g sugars, 15 g pro.

BREAKFAST FRENCH BREAD PIZZA

SUPER QUICK	MAKES 4 SERVINGS

1 8-oz. whole grain or regular baguette-style French bread, halved lengthwise

1½ cups shredded Swiss, Gouda, or Fontina cheese (6 oz.)

6 eggs

¼ cup milk

2 links cooked chicken sausage with apple, halved lengthwise and sliced

1 small zucchini, quartered lengthwise and sliced (1½ cups)

1 Tbsp. butter

1 Tbsp. chopped fresh chives (optional)

¼ tsp. crushed red pepper (optional)

1. Preheat broiler. Line a baking sheet with foil. Lay bread halves cut sides up on prepared baking sheet. Broil 4 to 5 inches from heat 1 to 2 minutes or until toasted. Top baguette halves with half of the cheese.

2. In a medium bowl beat together eggs and milk. In a large skillet cook sausage and zucchini in butter over medium-high 2 minutes. Reduce heat to medium. Add egg mixture and, if using, chives and red pepper. Cook, without stirring, until mixture begins to set on bottom and around edges. Using a spatula or large spoon, lift and fold partially cooked egg mixture so that uncooked portion flows underneath. Continue cooking 2 to 3 minutes or until egg mixture is cooked through but is still glossy and moist.

3. Spoon egg mixture over baguette halves. Top with the remaining cheese. Broil 4 to 5 inches from heat 1 to 2 minutes or until cheese melts. Cut into serving-size pieces.

EACH SERVING 555 cal., 31 g fat (14 g sat. fat), 370 mg chol., 879 mg sodium, 35 g carb., 4 g fiber, 5 g sugars, 34 g pro.

[MAKE A SWAP]

HERE'S A GOOD OPPORTUNITY TO USE UP PARTIAL PACKAGES IN THE REFRIGERATOR. ANY KIND OF CHEESE OR SAUSAGE WORKS WELL AS A TOPPING.

BACON-AND-EGGS OATMEAL BOWLS

INSTANT MEAL	MAKES 4 SERVINGS

Nonstick cooking spray
1½ cups steel-cut oats
½ tsp. salt
4½ cups water
2 tsp. butter
4 eggs
Black pepper (optional)
1 Tbsp. butter
½ cup shredded sharp cheddar cheese (2 oz.)
1 medium avocado, halved, seeded, peeled, and sliced
4 slices bacon, crisp-cooked and crumbled
2 Tbsp. thinly sliced green onion
Hot pepper sauce (optional)

1. Coat the inside of a 6-qt. multifunction electric or stove-top pressure cooker with cooking spray. Add oats and salt; stir in the water.

2. Lock lid in place. Set electric cooker on high pressure to cook 10 minutes. For stove-top cooker, bring up to pressure over medium-high; reduce heat enough to maintain steady (but not excessive) pressure. Cook 10 minutes. Remove from heat. For both models, let stand 15 minutes to release pressure naturally. Release any remaining pressure. Open lid carefully.

3. Meanwhile, in a large nonstick skillet melt the 2 tsp. butter over medium. Break eggs into skillet. If desired, sprinkle with pepper and additional salt. Reduce heat to low; cook eggs 3 to 4 minutes or until whites are set and yolks start to thicken. For over-easy fried eggs, turn eggs and cook 30 to 60 seconds more.

4. Stir the 1 Tbsp. butter into oats. Spoon oatmeal into bowls. Top with cheese, fried eggs, avocado, bacon, and green onion. If desired, serve with hot pepper sauce.

EACH SERVING 520 cal., 27 g fat (10 g sat. fat), 221 mg chol., 636 mg sodium, 48 g carb., 10 g fiber, 0 g sugars, 23 g pro.

Nutty Cherry-Apple Oatmeal Bowls Prepare as directed in Step 1, except stir 1 cup peeled and shredded apple and 1 tsp. Chinese five-spice powder into oat mixture. Cook as directed in Step 2. Stir ½ cup snipped dried cherries into oatmeal with the 1 Tbsp. butter; let stand 3 minutes. Omit fried eggs, avocado, cheese, bacon, green onion, and hot pepper sauce. Top servings with ¼ cup coarsely chopped toasted nuts and, if desired, drizzle with ¼ cup melted cherry jelly or pure maple syrup. Serve with milk.
EACH SERVING 420 cal.,13 g fat (3 g sat. fat), 8 mg chol., 325 mg sodium, 67 g carb., 10 g fiber, 18 g sugars, 12 g pro.

SMOKED SALMON WRAPS

HEALTHY	SUPER QUICK	MAKES 2 SERVINGS

1 small zucchini, trimmed

1 lemon

⅓ cup cream cheese spread

1 Tbsp. chopped fresh chives

4 6- to 7-inch whole wheat flour tortillas

3 oz. thinly sliced smoked salmon (lox-style), cut into strips

Lemon wedges (optional)

1. To make zucchini ribbons, draw a vegetable peeler lengthwise along the zucchini to cut very thin slices. Remove 1 tsp. zest and squeeze 1 Tbsp. juice from lemon. In a small bowl stir together lemon zest and juice, cream cheese spread, and chives until smooth. Spread cream cheese mixture evenly over tortillas, leaving a ½-inch border around edges.

2. Divide salmon among tortillas. Place zucchini ribbons on top of salmon. Roll up tortillas. Cut into pieces. If desired, serve with lemon wedges.

EACH SERVING 248 cal., 12 g fat (3 g sat. fat), 30 mg chol., 902 mg sodium, 28 g carb., 18 g fiber, 4 g sugars, 24 g pro.

ZUCCHINI AND TOMATO FRITTATA

MAKES 4 SERVINGS

8 eggs, lightly beaten
¼ tsp. salt
¼ tsp. crushed red pepper
1 Tbsp. olive oil
1 small zucchini, thinly sliced
½ cup yellow and/or red cherry tomatoes, halved
2 oz. bite-size fresh mozzarella balls
⅓ cup coarsely chopped walnuts

1. Preheat broiler. In a medium bowl combine eggs, salt, and crushed red pepper. In a large broilerproof skillet heat oil over medium-high. Place zucchini slices in skillet; cook 3 minutes, turning once. Top with tomatoes.

2. Pour egg mixture over zucchini mixture in skillet. Top with cheese and walnuts. Cook over medium 4 to 5 minutes or until egg mixture begins to set around edges, lifting mixture with a spatula so uncooked portion flows underneath.

3. Place skillet under broiler 4 inches from heat. Broil 2 to 3 minutes or until top is set.

EACH SERVING 281 cal., 22 g fat (6 g sat. fat), 382 mg chol., 334 mg sodium, 4 g carb., 1 g fiber, 2 g sugars, 17 g pro.

[FINISH WITH FLAVOR]

THINK FRESH AND SEASONAL. ADD A TUMBLE OF HALVED GRAPE TOMATOES AND FRESH BASIL LEAVES, THEN DRIZZLE WITH A LITTLE OLIVE OIL.

BAGEL AND LOX SKILLET STRATA

MAKES 6 SERVINGS

⅓ cup thinly sliced leek

1 Tbsp. unsalted butter

5 oz. fresh asparagus spears, trimmed and cut into pieces

5 eggs

1 cup whole milk

¾ cup crumbled feta cheese (3 oz.)

1 Tbsp. chopped fresh dill

¼ tsp. black pepper

8 oz. thinly sliced smoked salmon (lox-style), chopped

1 4-oz. plain bagel, toasted and cut into pieces

Crème fraîche and/or capers

1. Preheat oven to 450°F. In a large oven-going skillet cook and stir leek in melted butter over medium-high about 3 minutes or until tender. Add asparagus; cook 3 minutes more, stirring occasionally.

2. Meanwhile, in a medium bowl whisk together eggs, milk, cheese, dill, and pepper. Stir in salmon and bagel pieces. Pour egg mixture into skillet, stirring to combine. Cover with foil.

3. Bake 10 minutes. Remove foil. Bake, uncovered, 12 to 14 minutes more or until a knife comes out clean. Let stand 5 minutes. Serve with crème fraîche and/or capers or additional cheese and/or dill.

Tip To make your skillet ovenproof, wrap the handle in foil. This will reduce heating and convection.

EACH SERVING 279 cal., 15 g fat (8 g sat. fat), 204 mg chol., 774 mg sodium, 15 g carb., 1 g fiber, 5 g sugars, 20 g pro.

ASPARAGUS-EGG BREAKFAST SANDWICHES

HEALTHY	SUPER QUICK	MAKES 2 SERVINGS

4 slices whole wheat bread, toasted

Dijon-style mustard

1 avocado, halved, seeded, peeled, and mashed

8 to 12 fresh asparagus spears, steamed

1 hard-boiled egg, sliced

Coarse sea salt and cracked black pepper

1. Spread two bread slices with mustard. Spread remaining two bread slices with mashed avocado; top with asparagus and hard-boiled egg and sprinkle with salt and pepper. Top with mustard-coated bread.

EACH SERVING 383 cal., 15 g fat (2 g sat. fat), 93 mg chol., 523 mg sodium, 49 g carb., 12 g fiber, 10 g sugars, 16 g pro.

[SPEED IT UP]

GET A JUMP START ON THESE SANDWICHES BY STEAMING THE ASPARAGUS AND HARD-BOILING THE EGG AHEAD OF TIME. COVER AND CHILL ASPARAGUS UP TO 5 DAYS AND UNPEELED EGG UP TO 7 DAYS.

POACHED EGG BREAKFAST BOWLS

HEALTHY	MAKES 4 SERVINGS

1 Tbsp. cider vinegar

4 eggs

2 tsp. olive oil

2 cups sliced fresh button mushrooms

4 cups chopped fresh kale or spinach

1 15-oz. can cannellini (white kidney) beans, rinsed and drained

1 cup quartered grape tomatoes or ½ cup sliced oil-packed dried tomatoes

¼ tsp. salt or garlic salt

¼ tsp. lemon-pepper seasoning or black pepper

¼ cup chopped green onions (optional)

1. Add 4 cups water to a large skillet; add vinegar. Bring to simmering. Break an egg into a custard cup and slip egg into simmering water. Repeat with remaining eggs, allowing each egg an equal amount of space. Simmer 3 to 5 minutes or until whites are completely set and yolks start to thicken but are not hard. Using a slotted spoon, remove eggs from skillet and keep warm.

2. Empty skillet and wipe clean. In skillet heat oil over medium. Add mushrooms; cook 3 to 5 minutes or until tender, stirring occasionally. Add kale; cook about 30 seconds or until wilted, stirring frequently. Stir in beans, tomatoes, salt, and lemon-pepper seasoning; heat through.

3. Divide bean mixture among bowls. Top with poached eggs and, if desired, green onions.

EACH SERVING 219 cal., 8 g fat (2 g sat. fat), 186 mg chol., 469 mg sodium, 24 g carb., 8 g fiber, 4 g sugars, 16 g pro.

Mexican Serve breakfast bowls with salsa verde, queso fresco, plain low-fat yogurt, and/or chopped fresh cilantro.

Asian Serve breakfast bowls with kimchi, sriracha sauce, soy sauce, and/or toasted sesame oil.

Mediterranean Serve breakfast bowls with plain low-fat yogurt, crumbled feta cheese, and/or chopped fresh oregano.

Italian Serve breakfast bowls with chopped prosciutto, shredded Parmesan cheese, chopped fresh basil, and/or a drizzle of balsamic vinegar.

Southern Serve breakfast bowls with shredded cheddar cheese, light sour cream, and/or hot pepper sauce.

FRICO FRIED EGG AND CHEESE BREAKFAST SANDWICHES

SUPER QUICK	MAKES 4 SERVINGS

½ cup shredded Parmesan or Grana Padano cheese (2 oz.)

4 eggs
Salt and black pepper

4 slices provolone cheese

4 English muffins, split and toasted

¼ cup thinly sliced oil-packed dried tomatoes

1 cup baby arugula

1. Heat an extra-large griddle or nonstick skillet over low. Sprinkle Parmesan cheese into four 4-inch rounds onto hot griddle. Cook about 1 minute or just until cheese begins to melt.

2. Break eggs onto cheese rounds; sprinkle with salt and pepper. Cook 4 to 5 minutes or until egg whites are completely set and yolks are desired doneness. Top with provolone cheese; cook about 3 minutes or until melted.

3. Layer bottoms of English muffins with dried tomatoes. Add eggs, arugula, and tops of muffins. Serve immediately.

EACH SERVING 380 cal., 18 g fat (7 g sat. fat), 207 mg chol., 760 mg sodium, 35 g carb., 1 g fiber, 3 g sugars, 19 g pro.

[FINISH WITH FLAVOR]

LOOK IN YOUR REFRIGERATOR. SPREAD MUSTARD, AÏOLI, PESTO, OR ANY OTHER SANDWICH TOPPING ON THE ENGLISH MUFFINS BEFORE ASSEMBLING THESE SANDWICHES.

COTTAGE CHEESE BREAKFAST BOWL

HEALTHY	SUPER QUICK	MAKES 1 SERVING

¾ cup low-fat cottage cheese

¾ cup fresh raspberries, blueberries, and/or blackberries

¼ cup peeled and sliced kiwi fruit

¼ cup granola

2 Tbsp. snipped dried apricots

1 tsp. chia seeds

1. Spread cottage cheese in a wide, shallow bowl. Top with remaining ingredients.

EACH SERVING 481 cal., 15 g fat (3 g sat. fat), 7 mg chol., 704 mg sodium, 59 g carb., 13 g fiber, 33 g sugars, 30 g pro.

[MAKE A SWAP]

THERE ARE ENDLESS OPTIONS FOR TOPPING THIS BOWL. USE ANY FAVORITE FRESH OR DRIED FRUITS, MUESLI OR TOASTED NUTS FOR THE GRANOLA, AND FLAXSEEDS FOR THE CHIA SEEDS.

PINEAPPLE AND YOGURT BREAKFAST SUNDAES

HEALTHY	SUPER QUICK	MAKES 4 SERVINGS

1 whole medium fresh pineapple (about 3 lb.)

1 lime

1½ cups plain fat-free Greek yogurt

2 Tbsp. honey

1 cup fresh raspberries and/or blackberries

¼ cup chopped toasted walnuts or pepitas (pumpkin seeds)

2 Tbsp. large flaked unsweetened coconut, toasted

1. Using a sharp knife, cut off top and bottom of pineapple; cut off peel. Quarter pineapple lengthwise. Remove core from each pineapple quarter. Slice fruit crosswise into ¼-inch-thick slices.

2. Remove ½ tsp. zest and squeeze 2 tsp. juice from lime. In a bowl stir together lime peel and juice, yogurt, and honey. Spoon yogurt mixture into bowls. Top with pineapple, berries, walnuts, and coconut.

EACH SERVING 244 cal., 6 g fat (1 g sat. fat), 0 mg chol., 42 mg sodium, 41 g carb., 5 g fiber, 32 g sugars, 12 g pro.

[FINISH WITH FLAVOR]

GIVE THESE SUNDAES AN UNEXPECTED BURST OF CRYSTALLIZED GINGER, FIVE-SPICE POWDER, OR FRESHLY GRATED NUTMEG.

PEACHES AND CREAM BREAKFAST QUINOA

HEALTHY	INSTANT MEAL	MAKES 8 SERVINGS

4 cups water

2 cups uncooked white quinoa, rinsed and drained

3 cups chopped peeled fresh peaches or frozen sliced peaches, thawed

¼ cup peach preserves

2 tsp. vanilla

¾ tsp. salt

½ cup heavy cream

1. In a 4-qt. multifunction electric or stove-top pressure cooker combine the first six ingredients (through salt).

2. Lock lid in place. Set electric cooker on high pressure to cook 1 minute. For a stove-top cooker, bring up to pressure over medium-high; reduce heat enough to maintain steady (but not excessive) pressure. Cook 1 minute. Remove from heat. Let stand 15 minutes to release pressure naturally. Release any remaining pressure. Open lid carefully. Stir in cream.

EACH SERVING 261 cal., 8 g fat (4 g sat. fat), 17 mg chol., 231 mg sodium, 40 g carb., 4 g fiber, 10 g sugars, 7 g pro.

[FINISH WITH FLAVOR]

ADD A TOUCH OF SWEETNESS AND CRUNCH WITH A DRIZZLE OF HONEY AND SPRINKLING OF TOASTED PECANS. YOU CAN ALSO POUR A LITTLE MORE CREAM OR MILK OVER THE TOP.

STUFFED FRENCH TOAST WAFFLES

MAKES 4 SERVINGS

2 eggs, lightly beaten

½ cup milk

1 Tbsp. sugar

1 tsp. vanilla

4 1½-inch thick slices
brioche bread*

Fillings

Powdered sugar, pure maple
syrup, fruit preserves, honey,
or salsa

1. In a shallow bowl beat together eggs, milk, sugar, and vanilla. Cut horizontal pockets in bread slices. Stuff pockets with Fillings. Dip bread in the egg mixture, 10 seconds per side.

2. Add dipped bread to a preheated, lightly greased waffle baker. Close lid quickly; do not open until done. Bake according to manufacturer's directions. When done, use a fork to lift waffle off grid. Repeat with remaining stuffed bread. Top as desired.

*Tip Other rich egg breads such as challah, Hawaiian sweet bread, or brioche rolls (trim off tops and bottoms) may be used.

FILLINGS (FOR FOUR SLICES)

Chocolate-Banana ¼ cup chocolate hazelnut spread + 1 fresh banana, sliced
EACH SERVING 435 cal., 22 g fat (11 g sat. fat), 188 mg chol., 310 mg sodium, 50 g carb., 1 g fiber, 24 g sugars, 11 g pro.

Honey-Peach ¼ cup honey-nut cream cheese spread + ½ cup thinly sliced fresh peaches
EACH SERVING 349 cal., 20 g fat (11 g sat. fat), 195 mg chol., 354 mg sodium., 34 g carb., 0 g fiber, 11 g sugars, 10 g pro.

Strawberry-Mascarpone ¼ cup mascarpone cheese + ½ cup sliced fresh strawberries
EACH SERVING 338 cal., 20 g fat (10 g sat. fat), 197 mg chol., 306 mg sodium., 32 g carb., 0 g fiber, 9 g sugars, 10 g pro

Turkey-Pepper 4 slices (4 oz.) Monterey Jack cheese with jalapeño peppers + 4 oz. thinly sliced cooked turkey
EACH SERVING 443 cal., 26 g fat (14 g sat. fat), 223 mg chol., 730 mg sodium, 31 g carb., 0 g fiber, 8 g sugars, 20 g pro.

COTTAGE CHEESE PANCAKES

MAKES 4 SERVINGS

6 eggs, lightly beaten
1 16-oz. carton cottage cheese
2 Tbsp. honey
2 Tbsp. unsalted butter, melted
2 tsp. vanilla
1 tsp. lemon zest
1½ cups all-purpose flour
1 tsp. baking powder
1 tsp. baking soda
½ tsp. salt
Butter, pure maple syrup, and/or fresh berries

1. In a large bowl combine first six ingredients (through lemon zest). In a medium bowl combine flour, baking powder, baking soda, and salt. Add flour mixture to egg mixture. Stir just until moistened (batter should be slightly lumpy).

2. Pour about ¼ cup batter onto a hot, lightly greased griddle or heavy skillet. Cook over medium about 2 minutes or until surfaces are bubbly and edges are slightly dry; turn pancakes. Cook about 2 minutes more or until bottoms are browned. Keep warm in a 200°F oven while cooking remaining pancakes. Serve warm with butter, maple syrup, and/or fresh berries.

EACH SERVING 341 cal., 11 g fat (5 g sat. fat), 205 mg chol., 792 mg sodium, 43 g carb., 1 g fiber, 17 g sugars, 17 g pro.

WHOLE WHEAT CINNAMON-ROLL PANCAKES

MAKES 12 SERVINGS

⅓ cup packed brown sugar

1 Tbsp. cornstarch

1½ tsp. ground cinnamon

¼ cup butter, melted

1 cup all-purpose flour

¾ cup whole wheat flour

1 Tbsp. packed brown sugar

2 tsp. baking powder

½ tsp. baking soda

¼ tsp. salt

2 cups buttermilk or sour milk*

1 egg, lightly beaten

3 Tbsp. canola oil

1 recipe Cream Cheese Drizzle

1. For filling, in a bowl stir together the first four ingredients (through butter). Spoon mixture into a heavy resealable plastic bag.**

2. In another bowl stir together the next six ingredients (through salt). Make a well in center of flour mixture. In a third bowl use a fork to combine buttermilk, egg, and oil. Add egg mixture to flour mixture. Stir just until moistened (batter should be lumpy).

3. For each pancake, pour about ¼ cup batter onto a hot, lightly greased nonstick griddle or heavy skillet. Spread batter if necessary. Snip a very small piece off one of the corners of the bag with the filling. Starting from the center of pancake, squeeze a thin stream in a large swirl on top of the batter. Cook over medium 1 to 2 minutes per side or until golden brown (adjust heat as necessary to prevent cinnamon mixture from burning). Repeat with remaining batter and filling. Top pancakes with Cream Cheese Drizzle. Serve warm.

*Tip To make sour milk, place 1½ Tbsp. lemon juice or vinegar in a glass measuring cup. Add enough milk to make 1½ cups total liquid; stir. Let stand 5 minutes before using.

**Tip If filling separates while sitting, squeeze bag to mix it together before using.

Cream Cheese Drizzle In a bowl beat 3 oz. reduced-fat cream cheese (neufchatel) and ½ tsp. vanilla with an electric mixer on medium-high until creamy. Beat in 1 cup powdered sugar, adding milk as needed to make the icing drizzling consistency.

EACH SERVING 246 cal., 10 g fat (4 g sat. fat), 34 mg chol., 289 mg sodium, 34 g carb., 1 g fiber, 19 g sugars, 5 g pro.

BERRY BREAKFAST PIZZAS

MAKES 4 SERVINGS

¼ cup granulated sugar
4 tsp. cornstarch
Dash salt
½ cup water
2 cups mixed fresh berries, such as blueberries, raspberries, and/or blackberries
1 tsp. butter
1 tsp. orange zest
4 oz. reduced-fat cream cheese (neufchatel), softened
2 Tbsp. orange marmalade
2 tsp. granulated sugar
¼ tsp. ground cardamom, cinnamon, or apple pie spice
2 pita bread rounds, split
2 Tbsp. butter, melted
Powdered sugar (optional)

1. For berry topping, in a medium saucepan combine the first three ingredients (through salt). Stir in the water. Stir in ½ cup of the berries. Cook and stir over medium until thickened. Remove from heat. Add 1 cup of the remaining berries and the 1 tsp. butter, stirring until butter is melted. Gently stir in orange zest.

2. In a bowl beat cream cheese and orange marmalade with a mixer on low to medium until smooth. In another bowl stir together the 2 tsp. granulated sugar and the cardamom.

3. Toast the split pita rounds. Brush pita rounds with the 2 Tbsp. melted butter; sprinkle with the sugar-cardamom mixture. Spread cream cheese mixture on pita rounds; top with berry topping. Top with the remaining ½ cup berries. If desired, sprinkle with powdered sugar.

EACH SERVING 343 cal., 14 g fat (8 g sat. fat), 39 mg chol., 359 mg sodium, 51 g carb., 4 g fiber, 27 g sugars, 6 g pro.

To Make Ahead Make the berry topping as directed in Step 1; cool completely. Cover and chill up to 8 hours.

[MAKE A SWAP]

MIX UP THE FRUIT BY TOPPING PIZZAS WITH SLICED FRESH PEACHES OR PLUMS INSTEAD OF RESERVED FRESH BERRIES.

BEEF, PORK & LAMB

THE TRICK TO KEEPING MEAT ON THE MENU WHEN YOU'RE BUSY IS TO START WITH SMALL CUTS AND USE QUICK-COOKING METHODS. OPT FOR THINLY SLICED OR CUBED MEAT, GROUND MEAT, OR CHOPS IN STIR-FRIES, SKILLET MEALS, AND GRILLED SPECIALTIES. YOU CAN HAVE YOUR MEAT—AND EAT IT, TOO!.

BARBECUE BEEF STIR-FRY BOWLS

HEALTHY	MAKES 4 SERVINGS

¼ cup barbecue sauce

2 Tbsp. reduced-sodium soy sauce

1 Tbsp. packed brown sugar

2 tsp. Asian chili-garlic sauce

2 Tbsp. canola oil

1 8-oz. pkg. sliced fresh mushrooms

1½ cups packaged fresh julienned carrots

4 cups sliced bok choy (8 oz.)

1 lb. boneless beef sirloin steak, trimmed and cut into thin bite-size strips

Slivered red onion

1 8.5-oz. pkg. cooked basmati rice, heated according to package directions

1. In a small bowl stir together the first four ingredients (through chili-garlic sauce).

2. In a wok or extra-large nonstick skillet heat 1 Tbsp. of the oil over medium-high. Add mushrooms and carrots; cook and stir 4 minutes. Add bok choy; cook 2 minutes or until crisp-tender. Remove vegetables and any liquid from wok.

3. Add the remaining 1 Tbsp. oil to wok. Add beef; cook and stir 2 to 3 minutes or until beef is desired doneness. Return vegetables and any liquid to wok. Add sauce; toss to coat. Heat through. Top with red onion. Serve in shallow bowls over rice.

EACH SERVING 351 cal., 12 g fat (2 g sat. fat), 61 mg chol., 564 mg sodium, 36 g carb., 3 g fiber, 14 g sugars, 25 g pro.

SWEET AND SPICY EDAMAME-BEEF STIR-FRY

HEALTHY	MAKES 4 SERVINGS

4 tsp. vegetable oil

2 tsp. finely chopped fresh ginger

2 cups broccoli florets

1 cup red and/or yellow sweet pepper strips

8 oz. boneless beef sirloin steak, trimmed and cut into thin bite-size strips

1 cup frozen edamame

3 Tbsp. hoisin sauce

2 Tbsp. rice vinegar

1 tsp. red chili paste

2 cups hot cooked brown or white rice

1. In a nonstick wok or large skillet heat 2 tsp. of the oil over medium-high. Add ginger; cook and stir 15 seconds. Add broccoli and sweet pepper; cook and stir about 4 minutes or until crisp-tender. Remove vegetables from wok.

2. Add remaining 2 tsp. oil to wok. Add beef and edamame; cook and stir over medium-high 2 minutes or until beef is desired doneness. Return vegetables to wok.

3. In a bowl stir together hoisin sauce, vinegar, and chili paste. Add to wok, tossing to coat; heat through. Serve over rice.

EACH SERVING 340 cal., 11 g fat (2 g sat. fat), 24 mg chol., 262 mg sodium, 38 g carb., 6 g fiber, 8 g sugars, 22 g pro.

BIG BEEF BURRITOS

INSTANT MEAL	MAKES 6 SERVINGS

1½ lb. boneless beef sirloin steak, trimmed and cut into thin strips

1 large red sweet pepper, cut into strips

1 medium onion, cut into thin wedges

1 cup salsa

1 8.8-oz. pkg. cooked whole grain brown or Spanish rice blend

1 15-oz. can black or pinto beans, rinsed and drained

½ tsp. ground cumin

½ tsp. chili powder

¼ cup chopped fresh cilantro

6 10-inch flour tortillas

1½ cups crumbled queso fresco (6 oz.)

1. In a 6-qt. multifunction electric or stove-top pressure cooker combine the first four ingredients (through salsa); stir to coat.

2. Lock lid in place. Set cooker on high pressure to cook 5 minutes. For stove-top cooker, bring up to pressure over medium-high. Reduce heat enough to maintain steady (but not excessive) pressure. Cook 5 minutes. Remove from heat. For both models, release pressure quickly. Open lid carefully.

3. Meanwhile, heat rice according to package directions. In a medium bowl combine rice, beans, cumin, and chili powder. Microwave, covered, 1 to 2 minutes or until heated through, stirring once. Stir in cilantro.

4. Using tongs, place beef mixture on tortillas. Top with rice mixture and cheese. Fold bottom edges of tortillas over filling. Fold in opposite sides and roll up.

EACH SERVING 575 cal., 18 g fat (8 g sat. fat), 96 mg chol., 1,220 mg sodium, 62 g carb., 7 g fiber, 5 g sugars, 41 g pro.

[MAKE A SWAP]

GO FOR SHREDDED MEXICAN-STYLE FOUR-CHEESE BLEND OR MONTEREY JACK CHEESE WITH JALAPEÑOS INSTEAD OF THE QUESO FRESCO.

STEAKHOUSE SALAD PLATTER

MAKES 4 SERVINGS

12 oz. baby red and/or yellow potatoes, halved

2 cups fresh or frozen whole kernel corn

2 boneless beef shoulder top blade (flat iron) steaks, halved (1 to 1¼ lb. total)

2 tsp. barbecue seasoning

½ cup ranch salad dressing

2 Tbsp. barbecue sauce

6 cups chopped romaine lettuce

1 cup grape tomatoes, halved

½ cup slivered red onion

6 strips bacon, chopped and crisp-cooked

1. In a large saucepan combine potatoes and enough water to cover. Bring to boiling; reduce heat. Cover and simmer about 15 minutes or just until potatoes are tender, adding corn the last 2 minutes of cooking. Drain.

2. Meanwhile, lightly grease a grill pan. Preheat pan over medium-high. Sprinkle steaks on both sides with barbecue seasoning. Grill steaks in pan 8 to 12 minutes or until medium rare (145°F), turning once or twice. Remove steaks from pan. Cover with foil; let stand 5 minutes. Slice steak across grain.

3. In a bowl stir together salad dressing and barbecue sauce. On a platter arrange lettuce, cooked potatoes and corn, and steak. Top with tomatoes, red onion, and bacon. Serve with dressing.

EACH SERVING 551 cal., 27 g fat (7 g sat. fat), 123 mg chol., 821 mg sodium, 42 g carb., 5 g fiber, 10 g sugars, 40 g pro.

[MAKE A SWAP]

PARTIAL BOTTLES OF CHILI SAUCE OR COCKTAIL SAUCE CAN BE HARD TO USE UP. MIX THEM WITH THE RANCH DRESSING INSTEAD OF THE BARBECUE SAUCE.

PASTA WITH GARLICKY STEAK AND RED ONIONS

HEALTHY	MAKES 6 SERVINGS

12 oz. dried multigrain or tricolor penne pasta

2 Tbsp. olive oil

12 oz. boneless beef sirloin steak, trimmed and cut into thin bite-size pieces

1 medium red onion, quartered and thinly sliced

4 cloves garlic, minced

¾ tsp. salt

¼ tsp. crushed red pepper

1 cup reduced-sodium chicken broth

4 cups baby spinach

1 Tbsp. chopped fresh basil or thyme

¼ cup shaved Parmigiano-Reggiano cheese or Parmesan cheese (1 oz.) (optional)

1. Cook pasta in lightly salted water according to package directions. Drain, reserving ¼ cup of the pasta cooking water. Return pasta to hot pan; cover and keep warm.

2. In an extra-large nonstick skillet heat 1 Tbsp. of the oil over medium-high. Add meat; cook and stir 3 to 4 minutes or until meat is slightly pink in center. Remove from skillet; keep warm.

3. Add onion, garlic, salt, and crushed red pepper to skillet. Cook about 8 minutes or until onion is tender, stirring occasionally. Add broth and the reserved pasta cooking water; bring to boiling.

4. Add the remaining 1 Tbsp. oil, the meat, onion mixture, spinach, and basil to cooked pasta; toss just until spinach is wilted. If desired, sprinkle with cheese.

EACH SERVING 358 cal., 9 g fat (1 g sat. fat), 39 mg chol., 476 mg sodium, 45 g carb., 6 g fiber, 4 g sugars, 25 g pro.

[SPEED IT UP]

MULTITASKING SAVES TIME. WHILE THE PASTA COOKS, CUT THE STEAK INTO STRIPS AND COOK AS DIRECTED IN STEP 2.

ROASTED STEAK WITH TOMATOES AND MUSHROOMS

MAKES 4 SERVINGS

1 8-oz. pkg. sliced fresh mushrooms

1 pint red and/or yellow cherry or grape tomatoes

3 Tbsp. olive oil

1 Tbsp. balsamic vinegar

3 cloves garlic, minced

¼ tsp. salt

¼ tsp. black pepper

2 to 3 beef shoulder petite tenders (about 1½ lb. total) or 1½ lb. boneless beef top sirloin, cut 1½ inches thick

1 Tbsp. Montreal steak seasoning

2 to 3 tsp. chopped fresh oregano

Shaved Parmesan cheese (optional)

1. Preheat oven to 450°F. Line a 15×10-inch baking pan with foil. In the pan combine mushrooms, tomatoes, 1 Tbsp. of the olive oil, the vinegar, garlic, salt, and pepper. Toss to combine. Spread into an even layer. Roast about 15 minutes or until tomatoes are softened and mushrooms are tender.

2. Meanwhile, sprinkle meat all over with steak seasoning. In a large oven-going skillet heat the remaining 2 Tbsp. olive oil over medium-high. Add meat. Cook about 8 minutes or until well browned on all sides. Transfer skillet to oven. Roast 5 to 8 minutes or until medium rare (145°F). Transfer meat to cutting board; cover with foil and let stand 5 minutes. Slice meat.

3. Add oregano to tomato mixture; toss to combine. Serve with sliced steak. If desired, top with shaved Parmesan cheese and additional fresh oregano.

EACH SERVING 339 cal., 18 g fat (5 g sat. fat), 95 mg chol., 879 mg sodium, 5 g carb., 1 g fiber, 3 g sugars, 40 g pro.

SOUTHWESTERN NOODLE BOWL

HEALTHY	MAKES 8 SERVINGS

1½ lb. beef flank steak or beef top round steak, cut into thin bite-size strips

1 tsp. ground cumin

¼ tsp. salt

⅛ tsp. black pepper

2 Tbsp. canola oil

2 cloves garlic, minced

3 14.5-oz. cans reduced-sodium beef broth

4 oz. dried angel hair pasta, broken

1½ cups chopped red and/or yellow sweet peppers or frozen mixed vegetables

6 green onions, cut diagonally into 1-inch pieces

½ cup hot-style salsa

2 to 4 Tbsp. chopped fresh cilantro (optional)

1. Sprinkle meat with cumin, salt, and black pepper.

2. In a wok or extra-large skillet heat 1 Tbsp. of the oil over medium-high. Add garlic; cook and stir 15 seconds. Add half of the meat; cook and stir 2 to 3 minutes or until slightly pink in center. Remove from wok. Repeat with the remaining 1 Tbsp. oil and the remaining meat. Return all of the meat to the wok. Add broth; bring to boiling.

3. Stir in pasta, sweet peppers, and green onions; return to boiling. Cook about 4 minutes or until pasta is tender, stirring occasionally. Stir in the ½ cup salsa, and, if desired, cilantro; heat through. Serve with additional salsa.

EACH SERVING 229 cal., 9 g fat (2 g sat. fat), 53 mg chol., 424 mg sodium, 15 g carb., 1 g fiber, 3 g sugars, 22 g pro.

[MAKE A SWAP]

SUBSTITUTE SKINLESS, BONELESS CHICKEN BREAST FOR THE BEEF AND REDUCED-SODIUM CHICKEN BROTH FOR THE BEEF BROTH.

INDIAN-STYLE BEEF FAJITAS

HEALTHY	MAKES 4 SERVINGS

2 medium oranges

12 oz. beef skirt steak or flank steak

¾ tsp. ground cinnamon

¾ tsp. ground cumin

½ tsp. ground cardamom

⅛ tsp. cayenne pepper

Dash ground cloves

Nonstick cooking spray

2 medium red and/or yellow sweet peppers, stemmed, seeded, and cut into strips

1 cup sliced red onion

2 cloves garlic, minced

4 light oval multigrain wraps, halved and warmed

1 recipe Lime-Cilantro Yogurt Sauce

Lime wedges and/or orange wedges

1. Remove ½ tsp. zest from one of the oranges. Segment oranges, being careful to remove all of the white pith.

2. Very thinly slice meat across the grain into bite-size strips. In a bowl combine the next five ingredients (through cloves). Sprinkle spice mixture over meat, using your fingers to rub mixture into meat.

3. Coat an extra-large nonstick skillet with cooking spray. Heat skillet over medium-high. Add peppers, onion, and garlic; cook and stir about 4 minutes or until just tender. Remove vegetables from skillet.

4. Coat skillet with additional cooking spray. Add beef; cook and stir 2 to 3 minutes or until beef reaches desired doneness. Return vegetables to skillet. Gently stir in orange zest and orange segments. Remove from heat.

5. Spread wraps with Lime-Cilantro Yogurt Sauce. Top with beef and pepper mixture. Serve with lime and/or orange wedges.

Lime-Cilantro Yogurt Sauce In a bowl stir together ½ cup plain fat-free Greek yogurt, ¼ cup chopped fresh cilantro, 1 tsp. lime zest, and dash salt.

EACH SERVING *314 cal., 10 g fat (3 g sat. fat), 51 mg chol., 437 mg sodium, 34 g carb., 13 g fiber, 12 g sugars, 31 g pro.*

[MAKE A SWAP]

WARMED NAAN BREAD MAKES A GOOD STAND-IN FOR THE WRAPS IN THIS FUSION DISH.

MOLE-STYLE BEEF SOUP

HEALTHY	INSTANT MEAL	MAKES 6 SERVINGS

1 lb. lean ground beef

2 10-oz. cans diced tomatoes with green chiles, undrained

1 15-oz. can tomato sauce

1 14.5-oz. can reduced-sodium beef broth

1 cup chopped onion

1 cup chopped red or yellow sweet pepper

1 Tbsp. chili powder

1 Tbsp. packed brown sugar

2 tsp. unsweetened cocoa powder

2 tsp. dried oregano, crushed

½ tsp. ground cinnamon

2 cloves garlic, minced

Corn bread (optional)

1. Break beef into bite-size pieces and place in a 6-qt. multifunction electric or stove-top pressure cooker. Stir in the next 11 ingredients (through garlic).

2. Lock lid in place. Set electric cooker on high pressure to cook 5 minutes. For stove-top cooker, bring up to pressure over medium-high; reduce heat enough to maintain steady (but not excessive) pressure. Cook 5 minutes. Remove from heat. For both models, let stand 15 minutes to release pressure naturally. Release any remaining pressure. Open lid carefully. If desired, serve with corn bread.

EACH SERVING 194 cal., 6 g fat (2 g sat. fat), 48 mg chol., 955 mg sodium, 17 g carb., 4 g fiber, 9 g sugars, 19 g pro.

[FINISH WITH FLAVOR]

TOP THIS BEEFY SOUP AS YOU WOULD CHILI. SERVE WITH CRUMBLED QUESO FRESCO, SOUR CREAM, SLICED GREEN ONIONS, FRESH CILANTRO, ROASTED POBLANOS, AND/OR LIME WEDGES.

PASTA WITH BEEF-FENNEL RAGU

| HEALTHY | INSTANT MEAL | MAKES 8 SERVINGS |

- 1 lb. extra-lean ground beef
- 2 14.5-oz. cans diced tomatoes with basil, garlic, and oregano, undrained
- 2 cups thinly sliced fennel bulb
- 2 cups reduced-sodium chicken broth
- 1 15-oz. can tomato sauce
- ⅓ cup chopped onion
- 4 cloves garlic, minced
- 1½ tsp. fennel seeds, lightly crushed
- 1 tsp. dried oregano, crushed
- ½ tsp. black pepper
- ¼ tsp. salt
- 1 12-oz. pkg. no-boil, no-drain penne pasta
- ½ cup chopped fresh basil

1. Break ground beef into bite-size pieces and place in a 6-qt. electric or stove-top pressure cooker. Add the next 11 ingredients (through pasta). Stir to combine. Lock lid in place. Set electric cooker on high pressure to cook 2 minutes. For a stove-top cooker, bring up to pressure over medium-high; reduce heat enough to maintain steady (but not excessive) pressure. Cook 2 minutes. Remove from heat. For both models, let stand 5 minutes to release pressure naturally. Release any remaining pressure. Open lid carefully.

2. If desired, let stand, covered, up to 10 minutes for pasta to reach desired doneness. Top with basil.

EACH SERVING 304 cal., 5 g fat (2 g sat. fat), 36 mg chol., 807 mg sodium, 46 g carb., 4 g fiber, 9 g sugars, 20 g pro.

SKILLET BURGERS WITH SHALLOT-HERB BUTTER

MAKES 4 SERVINGS

3   Tbsp. finely chopped shallot
3   Tbsp. butter, softened
2   Tbsp. chopped Italian parsley
½   tsp. snipped fresh thyme
½   tsp. lemon zest
1½ lb. lean ground beef
½   tsp. salt
¼   tsp. black pepper
8   oz. shiitake mushrooms, stemmed and sliced
1   Tbsp. olive oil
4   slices Swiss cheese
4   ciabatta rolls, split, or 8 slices small, firm square bread (such as English muffin toasting bread), toasted

1. In a small bowl stir together the first five ingredients (through lemon zest) until well combined. Shape beef into four patties about ½ inch larger than the bread. Season patties with salt and pepper.

2. Heat an extra-large heavy skillet over medium-high. Add 1 Tbsp. butter mixture to pan and let melt. Add mushrooms; cook and stir about 3 minutes or just until tender. Transfer mushrooms to a bowl.

3. Add oil to skillet. When hot but not smoking, add patties to skillet. Cook about 3 minutes or until browned and slightly charred. Turn and cook about 3 minutes more or until done (160°F). Top patties with cheese. Cover and cook about 1 minute or until cheese is melted.

4. Meanwhile, spread remaining butter mixture on rolls. Fill rolls with burgers and mushroom mixture.

EACH SERVING 777 cal., 52 g fat (21 g sat. fat), 160 mg chol., 818 mg sodium, 36 g carb., 3 g fiber, 4 g sugars, 41 g pro.

SPICY MUSHROOM SLOPPY JOES

MAKES 6 SERVINGS

- 1 lb. extra-lean ground beef
- 1 8-oz. pkg. sliced fresh cremini or button mushrooms
- 2 cloves garlic, minced
- 1 8-oz. can tomato sauce
- ½ cup reduced-sodium beef broth
- 2 Tbsp. Worcestershire sauce
- 2 Tbsp. red wine vinegar
- 1 Tbsp. molasses
- ½ to ¾ tsp. ground chipotle chile pepper
- 6 multigrain hamburger buns, split and toasted
- 6 slices Monterey Jack cheese with jalapeño peppers or cheddar cheese
- Sliced red onion

1. In a large skillet cook beef, mushrooms, and garlic over medium-high until meat is browned. Drain off fat.

2. Stir in the next six ingredients (through chipotle pepper). Bring to boiling; reduce heat. Simmer, uncovered, 5 to 6 minutes or until liquid is slightly thickened (mixture should still be saucy). Serve in buns with cheese and onion.

EACH SERVING 330 cal., 13 g fat (6 g sat. fat), 66 mg chol., 655 mg sodium, 28 g carb., 3 g fiber, 9 g sugars, 27 g pro.

[MAKE A SWAP]
LOSE THE HAMBURGER BUNS AND SERVE THE BEEF MIXTURE OVER BAKED RUSSET OR SWEET POTATOES.

PHILLY CHEESESTEAK QUESADILLAS

MAKES 4 SERVINGS

1 lb. extra-lean ground beef

¾ cup chopped onion

¾ cup chopped green sweet pepper

½ cup sliced pepperoncini or mild cherry peppers, drained

2 Tbsp. Worcestershire sauce

1 tsp. dried oregano or parsley, crushed

½ tsp. black pepper

4 8-inch flour tortillas

Nonstick cooking spray

6 to 8 slices provolone cheese (6 to 8 oz. total)

1. In a large skillet cook and stir the first seven ingredients (through black pepper) over medium-high about 8 minutes or until meat is browned.

2. Lightly coat one side of tortillas with cooking spray. Place on work surface coated sides down. Place half of the cheese slices on half of each tortilla, tearing cheese to fit. Top with beef mixture and the remaining cheese. Fold unfilled halves of tortillas over top.

3. Heat an extra-large skillet or griddle over medium. Cook quesadillas, two at a time, 6 to 8 minutes or until cheese is melted and tortillas are lightly browned, turning once.

EACH SERVING 509 cal., 20 g fat (11 g sat. fat), 124 mg chol., 1,115 mg sodium, 33 g carb., 1 g fiber, 3 g sugars, 47 g pro.

[MAKE A SWAP]

GO ITALIAN BY USING BULK ITALIAN SAUSAGE FOR THE BEEF AND 1 TABLESPOON BALSAMIC VINEGAR FOR THE WORCESTERSHIRE SAUCE.

SKILLET LASAGNA

HEALTHY	MAKES 5 SERVINGS

Nonstick cooking spray
- 8 oz. extra-lean ground beef
- ¾ cup chopped green, red, or yellow sweet pepper
- ½ cup chopped onion
- 2 cloves garlic, minced
- 1 23.5-oz. jar pasta sauce
- 1 cup water
- 2 cups sliced fresh mushrooms
- 3 cups dried wide egg noodles
- ½ cup ricotta cheese
- 2 Tbsp. grated Parmesan or Romano cheese
- ½ tsp. dried Italian seasoning, crushed
- ½ cup shredded part-skim mozzarella cheese (2 oz.)

1. Coat an extra-large nonstick skillet with cooking spray; heat skillet over medium. Cook beef, sweet pepper, onion, and garlic in hot skillet until meat is browned, stirring occasionally. Drain off any fat. Stir in pasta sauce and the water. Bring to boiling. Add mushrooms and uncooked noodles; stir to separate noodles. Return to boiling; reduce heat. Cover and gently boil about 10 minutes or until pasta is tender, stirring occasionally.

2. Meanwhile, in a bowl stir together ricotta, Parmesan, and Italian seasoning. Drop cheese mixture by spoonfuls into 10 small mounds (about 1 Tbsp. each) on top of pasta mixture in skillet. Sprinkle each mound with mozzarella. Reduce heat to low. Cook, covered, 4 to 5 minutes or until cheese mixture is heated and mozzarella is melted. Serve immediately.

EACH SERVING 306 cal., 10 g fat (4 g sat. fat), 66 mg chol., 748 mg sodium, 32 g carb., 4 g fiber, 9 g sugars, 23 g pro.

KOREAN BEEF CABBAGE WRAPS

HEALTHY	SUPER QUICK	MAKES 4 SERVINGS

- 12 oz. extra-lean ground beef
- 3 Tbsp. reduced-sodium soy sauce
- 1 Tbsp. Asian garlic-chili sauce
- 2 tsp. toasted sesame oil
- 1 12-oz. pkg. shredded broccoli slaw mix
- 8 small napa or savoy cabbage leaves
- ½ cup chopped red sweet pepper

1. In an extra-large skillet cook beef over medium-high until browned. Drain off any fat. Add soy sauce, Asian chili sauce, and sesame oil to meat; stir to combine. Stir in slaw mix. Cook and stir over medium 2 to 3 minutes or until cooked through and slaw mixture is just wilted.

2. If using napa cabbage, trim each stem so you use the top leafy part of the cabbage. Spoon beef mixture onto the cabbage leaves. Top each with sweet pepper. Fold cabbage leaves around filling. Serve immediately.

EACH SERVING 185 cal., 7 g fat (2 g sat. fat), 53 mg chol., 567 mg sodium, 9 g carb., 3 g fiber, 5 g sugars, 21 g pro.

[FINISH WITH FLAVOR]

KOREAN DISHES USUALLY HAVE A SPICY FLAVOR. DRIZZLE SOME SRIRACHA SAUCE IN THESE WRAPS TO GET A KICK.

BEEF AND BLUE CHEESE SALAD WITH HONEY-HORSERADISH DRESSING

HEALTHY	MAKES 4 SERVINGS

6 cups torn romaine lettuce

2 heads Belgian endive, trimmed and thinly sliced crosswise

2 cups cooked, cooled quinoa*

6 oz. deli-style thinly sliced cooked roast beef

1 8-oz. pkg. steamed baby beets, cut into thin slices

2 medium apples, quartered, cored, and thinly sliced

⅓ cup chopped walnuts, toasted

¼ cup crumbled blue cheese

1 recipe Honey-Horseradish Dressing

1. Divide romaine and endive among plates. Spoon quinoa over greens. Top with the next five ingredients (through blue cheese). Drizzle with Honey-Horseradish Dressing.

*Tip To cook quinoa, in a medium saucepan combine ⅔ cup uncooked quinoa, rinsed and drained, and 1⅓ cups water. Bring to boiling; reduce heat. Cover and simmer 15 to 18 minutes or until quinoa is tender and liquid is absorbed. Spread quinoa in a shallow baking pan to cool.

Honey-Horseradish Dressing In a small bowl whisk together 3 Tbsp. light mayonnaise, 1 Tbsp. each lemon juice and honey, and 1 tsp. prepared horseradish until smooth.

EACH SERVING 380 cal., 14 g fat (3 g sat. fat), 30 mg chol., 765 mg sodium, 49 g carb., 9 g fiber, 22 g sugars, 17 g pro.

AUTUMN APPLES AND PORK

HEALTHY	INSTANT MEAL	MAKES 6 SERVINGS

1 1½-lb. pork tenderloin
¼ tsp. salt
¼ tsp. black pepper
1 Tbsp. canola oil
3 medium shallots, peeled and quartered lengthwise
⅓ cup apple cider or apple juice
2 Tbsp. cider vinegar
3 sprigs fresh thyme and/or fresh sage
3 tart red apples, unpeeled, cored, and thinly sliced
3 cups hot cooked buttered spaetzle or noodles

1. Sprinkle pork with salt and pepper. In a 6-qt. multifunction electric or stove-top pressure cooker cook pork in hot oil about 4 minutes or until browned. (For electric cooker, use sauté setting.) Add the next four ingredients (through thyme).

2. Lock lid in place. Set electric cooker on high pressure to cook 2 minutes. For stove-top cooker, bring up to pressure over medium-high; reduce heat enough to maintain steady (but not excessive) pressure. Cook 2 minutes. Remove from heat. For both models, let stand 10 minutes to release pressure naturally. Carefully release any remaining pressure. Open lid carefully. Remove and discard herb sprigs.

3. Transfer pork to a cutting board; cover. Return pressure cooker to heat and bring to a simmer; add apples. (For electric cooker, use sauté setting.) Cook, stirring occasionally, about 5 minutes or until apples are tender.

4. Slice pork into 12 slices and serve with spaetzle. Using a slotted spoon, spoon apples and shallots over pork. Garnish with additional fresh thyme and/or sage.

EACH SERVING 346 cal., 8 g fat (2 g sat. fat), 102 mg chol., 168 mg sodium, 38 g carb., 4 g fiber, 14 g sugars, 28 g pro.

GARLIC PORK AND SWEET POTATO HASH

HEALTHY	MAKES 4 SERVINGS

4 cups chopped sweet potatoes

1½ lb. pork tenderloin, trimmed and cut into ½-inch slices

2 Tbsp. reduced-sodium beef broth

½ tsp. sea salt

¼ tsp. black pepper

3 Tbsp. olive oil

8 cloves garlic, thinly sliced

¼ cup sliced green onions

2 Tbsp. honey

2 Tbsp. water

2 tsp. Dijon-style mustard
Chopped fresh thyme

1. Place sweet potatoes in a bowl; cover with vented plastic wrap. Microwave 8 minutes, stirring once. Remove plastic wrap; set potatoes aside. Brush pork with 1 Tbsp. of the broth and sprinkle with salt and pepper.

2. In an extra-large skillet heat oil over medium-high. Add garlic; cook and stir just until starting to turn golden.* Remove from skillet. Add meat; cook 4 to 6 minutes or until slightly pink in center, turning once. Remove from skillet; keep warm.

3. For hash, add sweet potatoes to skillet. Cook until starting to crisp, stirring occasionally. Add green onions; cook and stir 1 minute more. Season to taste with salt and pepper. Spoon hash onto plates; top with meat and garlic.

4. In the same skillet whisk together honey, the water, mustard, and remaining 1 Tbsp. broth. Cook and stir until bubbly; drizzle over meat. Sprinkle with thyme.

***Tip** Cook garlic just until golden but not too brown. If it burns, it will taste bitter.

EACH SERVING 433 cal., 14 g fat (3 g sat. fat), 111 mg chol., 516 mg sodium, 38 g carb., 4 g fiber, 14 g sugars, 38 g pro.

BANH MI SANDWICHES

HEALTHY	MAKES 6 SERVINGS

b/c not great (handwritten)

12 oz. pork tenderloin, trimmed and cut into ½-inch slices

1 to 2 Tbsp. sriracha or Asian sweet chili sauce

1 Tbsp. reduced-sodium soy sauce

Nonstick cooking spray

1 small cucumber, seeded and cut into thin strips

1 small red sweet pepper, cut into thin strips

½ cup shredded carrot

¼ cup chopped green onions

1 10-oz. loaf baguette-style French bread, split horizontally

1 recipe Sriracha Mayonnaise

¼ cup fresh cilantro leaves

1 fresh jalapeño chile pepper, thinly sliced and, if desired, seeded*

1. Lightly press meat slices to an even thickness. In a small bowl combine sriracha sauce and soy sauce; brush over meat. Coat a grill pan or extra-large skillet with cooking spray. Add meat; cook over medium-high 4 to 6 minutes or until slightly pink in center, turning once.

2. In a large bowl combine cucumber, sweet pepper, carrot, and green onions.

3. Spread bread with Sriracha Mayonnaise. Layer meat, vegetable mixture, cilantro, and jalapeño pepper between bread halves. Cut into portions.

*Tip Chile peppers contain oils that can irritate your skin and eyes. Wear plastic or rubber gloves when working with them.

Sriracha Mayonnaise In a small bowl combine ⅓ cup mayonnaise and 2 to 3 tsp. sriracha or Asian sweet chili sauce.

EACH SERVING 220 cal., 4 g fat (0 g sat. fat), 37 mg chol., 481 mg sodium, 26 g carb., 6 g fiber, 4 g sugars, 19 g pro.

[SPEED IT UP]
SWING BY THE SALAD BAR AT THE SUPERMARKET AND FILL A CONTAINER WITH ALREADY-PREPPED VEGGIES.

PORK RHUBARB SKILLET

HEALTHY	MAKES 4 SERVINGS

1 Tbsp. vegetable oil

1 lb. lean boneless pork, cut into bite-size strips

1 medium onion, cut into thin wedges

1½ cups sliced fresh rhubarb

1 medium cooking apple, cored and sliced

1 cup chicken broth

2 Tbsp. packed brown sugar

1 Tbsp. cornstarch

1 Tbsp. chopped fresh sage

½ tsp. salt

¼ tsp. black pepper

1⅓ cups hot cooked couscous

1. In an extra-large skillet heat oil over medium-high. Add pork; cook and stir 3 to 4 minutes or until browned. Remove pork from skillet.

2. Add onion; cook and stir 2 to 3 minutes or until tender. Add fresh rhubarb (if using) and apple; cook 3 to 4 minutes or until crisp-tender, stirring occasionally.

3. For sauce, in a bowl stir together the next six ingredients (through pepper). Add broth mixture and thawed frozen rhubarb (if using) to skillet; cook and stir until thickened and bubbly. Stir in meat; heat through. Serve over hot cooked couscous. If desired, garnish with additional fresh sage.

EACH SERVING 342 cal., 11 g fat (3 g sat. fat), 64 mg chol., 565 mg sodium, 32 g carb., 3 g fiber, 13 g sugars, 28 g pro.

[**SPEED IT UP**]

IF FRESH RHUBARB IS NOT IN SEASON OR IF YOU WANT TO SKIP THE CLEANING AND SLICING, USE FROZEN UNSWEETENED SLICED RHUBARB, THAWED.

MAPLE-PORK WILTED SALAD

HEALTHY	MAKES 4 SERVINGS

8 cups baby spinach or torn spinach

1½ cups peeled, seeded, and chopped cucumber

⅓ cup thin wedges red onion

12 oz. pork tenderloin, trimmed and cut into ¼-inch slices

¼ tsp. sea salt

¼ tsp. black pepper

2 Tbsp. olive oil

2 Tbsp. finely chopped shallot

¼ cup cider vinegar

¼ cup pure maple syrup

¼ cup sliced almonds, toasted

1. In a large bowl combine spinach, cucumber, and onion. Sprinkle pork with salt and pepper.

2. In a large skillet heat 1 Tbsp. of the oil over medium-high. Add pork; cook 2 to 3 minutes or just until slightly pink in center, turning once. Add pork to spinach mixture.

3. For dressing, in skillet heat the remaining 1 Tbsp. oil over medium. Add shallot; cook and stir about 2 minutes or until tender. Stir in vinegar and maple syrup. Simmer, uncovered, 1½ to 2 minutes or until slightly thickened. Season to taste with additional salt and pepper.

4. Pour dressing over spinach mixture; toss to coat. Top with almonds.

EACH SERVING 265 cal., 11 g fat (2 g sat. fat), 55 mg chol., 234 mg sodium, 20 g carb., 3 g fiber, 14 g sugars, 21 g pro.

TOMATO-PARMESAN PORK AND NOODLES

MAKES 4 SERVINGS

1 Tbsp. canola oil

12 oz. lean boneless pork, cut into 1-inch pieces

¾ cup reduced-sodium chicken broth

½ cup quartered grape tomatoes

¼ cup finely chopped shallot or onion

¼ cup heavy cream

1 Tbsp. butter

¼ cup finely shredded Parmesan cheese

  Salt and black pepper

2 oz. dried angel hair pasta

1 12-oz. pkg. refrigerated zucchini spirals (3 cups)

¼ cup chopped fresh basil

1. In a large skillet heat oil over medium-high. Reduce heat to medium. Add pork to skillet; cook 3 to 4 minutes or just until pink in the center. Remove from skillet.

2. Add broth, tomatoes, and shallot to skillet. Cook and stir over medium-high to scrape up browned bits from bottom of skillet. Bring to boiling; boil gently, uncovered, about 5 minutes or until liquid is reduced to ½ cup. Stir in cream, butter, and 2 Tbsp. of the Parmesan; cook about 3 minutes or until sauce is slightly thickened, stirring frequently. Return pork to skillet; heat through. Season to taste with salt and pepper.

3. Meanwhile, cook pasta according to package directions. Place zucchini spirals in colander. Pour pasta and cooking water over zucchini; drain. Lightly toss pasta mixture and transfer to plates. Top with pork mixture. Top with the remaining 2 Tbsp. Parmesan and basil.

EACH SERVING *310 cal., 16 g fat (7 g sat. fat), 82 mg chol., 424 mg sodium, 17 g carb., 2 g fiber, 5 g sugars, 26 g pro.*

THAI PORK WRAPS

HEALTHY	MAKES 6 SERVINGS

6 8- to 10-inch vegetable-flavor flour tortillas or plain flour tortillas
½ tsp. garlic salt
¼ to ½ tsp. black pepper
12 oz. pork tenderloin, cut into 1-inch strips
1 Tbsp. vegetable oil
4 cups shredded broccoli (broccoli slaw mix)
1 medium red onion, cut into thin wedges
1 tsp. grated fresh ginger
1 recipe Peanut Sauce

1. Preheat oven to 350°F. Wrap tortillas in foil. Bake about 10 minutes or until warm. Meanwhile, in a medium bowl combine garlic salt and pepper. Add pork; toss to coat.

2. In a large skillet cook and stir pork in hot oil over medium-high 4 to 6 minutes or until no longer pink. (Reduce heat if necessary to prevent overbrowning.) Remove pork from skillet; keep warm. Add broccoli, onion, and ginger to skillet. Cook and stir 4 to 6 minutes or until vegetables are crisp-tender. Remove from heat.

3. Spread Peanut Sauce over tortillas. Top with pork strips and vegetable mixture. Roll up tortillas, securing with toothpicks as needed. Serve immediately.

Peanut Sauce In a small saucepan combine ¼ cup creamy peanut butter, 3 Tbsp. water, 1 Tbsp. sugar, 2 tsp. soy sauce, and 1 clove garlic, minced. Heat over medium-low, whisking constantly, until smooth and warm. Use immediately or keep warm over very low heat, stirring occasionally.

EACH SERVING 383 cal., 13 g fat (3 g sat. fat), 37 mg chol., 661 mg sodium, 44 g carb., 5 g fiber, 6 g sugars, 22 g pro.

[MAKE A SWAP]
THESE FLAVORS GO PERFECTLY WITH CHICKEN, TOO. SUBSTITUTE 12 OUNCES SKINLESS, BONELESS CHICKEN BREAST STRIPS FOR THE PORK.

GREEN CHILE POSOLE

HEALTHY	INSTANT MEAL	MAKES 6 SERVINGS

1½ lb. boneless pork chops, trimmed and cut into ½-inch cubes

2 15- to 16-oz. cans yellow hominy, rinsed and drained

3 cups reduced-sodium chicken broth

1 16-oz. jar salsa verde

1 cup chopped onion

1 4-oz. can diced green chiles

1 tsp. ground cumin

2 cloves garlic, minced

1. In a 6-qt. multifunction electric or stove-top pressure cooker combine all the ingredients.

2. Lock lid in place. Set electric cooker on high pressure 5 minutes. For stove-top cooker, bring to pressure over medium-high. Reduce heat enough to maintain steady (but not excessive pressure). Cook 5 minutes. Remove from heat. For both models, release pressure quickly. Open lid carefully.

EACH SERVING 308 cal., 5 g fat (1 g sat. fat), 64 mg chol., 1,954 mg sodium, 32 g carb., 4 g fiber, 10 g sugars, 37 g pro.

[FINISH WITH FLAVOR]

SPRINKLE BOWLS OF POSOLE WITH CRUMBLED COTIJA CHEESE, SALTED ROASTED PEPITAS (PUMPKIN SEEDS), AND/OR CHOPPED FRESH CILANTRO.

GINGER PORK WITH SWEET PEPPERS

MAKES 4 SERVINGS

1 Tbsp. toasted sesame oil

1 lb. ground pork

2 Tbsp. chopped fresh ginger

6 cloves garlic, minced

2 cups red sweet pepper strips

⅓ cup water

⅓ cup reduced-sodium
soy sauce

2 tsp. packed brown sugar

2 cups hot cooked rice

½ cup chopped dry-roasted
peanuts

Chopped fresh basil
(optional)

1. In an extra-large skillet heat sesame oil over medium-high. Add ground pork, 1 Tbsp. of the ginger, and half of the garlic. Cook and stir until meat is browned and crispy. Remove from skillet.

2. Add peppers to skillet. Cook, without stirring, 2 to 3 minutes or until peppers begin to blacken and blister. Stir peppers; stir in the remaining ginger and garlic, the water, soy sauce, and brown sugar. Reduce heat to medium. Cook, covered, about 2 minutes more or until peppers are crisp-tender. Return meat to skillet. Cook and stir until heated through. Serve with rice and top with peanuts and, if desired, basil.

EACH SERVING 543 cal., 31 g fat (8 g sat. fat), 77 mg chol., 819 mg sodium, 37 g carb., 3 g fiber, 8 g sugars, 29 g pro.

[MAKE A SWAP]

MILD-FLAVOR GROUND PORK CAN BE REPLACED WITH GROUND TURKEY OR GROUND CHICKEN BREAST.

PORK AND DOUBLE BEAN STIR-FRY

¼ cup reduced-sodium chicken broth or water

3 Tbsp. reduced-sodium soy sauce

2 Tbsp. rice vinegar

2 tsp. Asian chili-garlic paste

1 tsp. packed brown sugar

1 Tbsp. vegetable oil

1 lb. ground pork

1 lb. thin green beans, trimmed

1 cup frozen shelled edamame

1 Tbsp. water

2 cups hot cooked brown or white basmati rice

Slivered red onion (optional)

Crushed red pepper (optional)

1. In a bowl stir together the first five ingredients (through brown sugar).

2. In an extra-large skillet heat oil over medium-high; add pork and press flat to make one large patty. Cook 3 to 4 minutes, without stirring. When pork is browned and crisp on bottom, break up the patty and stir in sauce. Cook and stir 2 to 3 minutes more or until pork is completely cooked and crumbled. Meanwhile, in a covered dish microwave beans, edamame, and the 1 Tbsp. water 3 to 4 minutes or until crisp-tender, stirring once; drain.

3. Add beans and edamame to pork mixture; toss to combine. Serve with rice. If desired, top with red onion and sprinkle with crushed red pepper.

EACH SERVING 484 cal., 24 g fat (6 g sat. fat), 77 mg chol., 508 mg sodium, 39 g carb., 6 g fiber, 7 g sugars, 30 g pro.

BLACK BEAN AND VEGETABLE SOUP WITH PROSCIUTTO GREMOLATA

HEALTHY	MAKES 6 SERVINGS

1 Tbsp. olive oil

½ of a 14.4-oz. pkg. (2 cups) frozen sweet pepper and onion stir-fry vegetables

1 32-oz. carton reduced-sodium chicken broth

2 15-oz. cans reduced-sodium black beans, rinsed and drained

1 10-oz. sweet potato, peeled and cut into ½-inch pieces

1 14.5-oz. can no-salt-added fire-roasted diced tomatoes, undrained

2 tsp. hot chili powder or berbere seasoning

Salt and black pepper

1 recipe Prosciutto Gremolata

1. In a 4-qt. Dutch oven heat oil over medium-high. Add frozen vegetables; cook 3 minutes, stirring occasionally. Stir in next five ingredients (through chili powder).

2. Bring to boiling; reduce heat. Simmer, covered, 15 minutes or until sweet potato is tender, stirring occasionally. Season to taste with salt and pepper. Top servings with Prosciutto Gremolata.

Prosciutto Gremolata Place 2 thin slices prosciutto between paper towels and set on a plate. Microwave 1 minute; cool and crumble. In a small bowl combine prosciutto, ¼ cup chopped fresh parsley, 2 tsp. lemon zest, and 1 clove garlic, minced.

EACH SERVING 230 cal., 3 g fat (0 g sat. fat), 1 mg chol., 769 mg sodium, 39 g carb., 9 g fiber, 6 g sugars, 12 g pro.

[SPEED IT UP]

CHECK OUT THE FREEZER SECTION FOR A 10-OUNCE PACKAGE OF CUBED SWEET POTATOES AND SAVE THE TIME OF PEELING AND CUTTING.

AVOCADO BLT CLUB SANDWICHES

MAKES 4 SERVINGS

1 ripe avocado
2 Tbsp. light mayonnaise
1 tsp. lemon juice
1 clove garlic, minced
8 thick slices multigrain country-style bread, toasted
4 oz. thinly sliced cooked turkey
4 oz. thinly sliced cooked ham
4 slices bacon, crisp-cooked and halved crosswise
4 leaves romaine lettuce
1 tomato, thinly sliced

1. Halve, seed, and peel avocado. In a small bowl mash one of the avocado halves; stir in mayonnaise, lemon juice, and garlic. Thinly slice remaining avocado half.

2. Layer four of the bread slices with the remaining ingredients. Spread remaining four bread slices with mashed avocado mixture; place on sandwiches.

EACH SERVING 311 cal., 13 g fat (3 g sat. fat), 9 mg chol., 953 mg sodium, 29 g carb., 7 g fiber, 6 g sugars, 20 g pro.

[SPEED IT UP]
PURCHASED COOKED BACON IS A QUICK SUB TO USE IN THESE SANDWICHES OR IN ANY RECIPE THAT CALLS FOR CRISP-COOKED BACON.

POTATO, BACON, AND ARUGULA PIZZA

MAKES 4 SERVINGS

3 slices bacon, chopped
1¼ cups ⅛-inch-thick slices Yukon gold or red potatoes
⅓ cup ⅛-inch slices onion
1 tsp. chopped fresh rosemary
½ tsp. salt
½ tsp. freshly ground black pepper
1 12-inch purchased thin pizza crust
1 tsp. olive oil
1 lemon
3 Tbsp. olive oil
¼ tsp. Dijon-style mustard
1 5-oz. pkg. baby arugula
¼ cup grated Parmesan cheese

1. Preheat oven to 450°F; reduce oven temperature to 425°F. In a large skillet cook bacon over medium just until it begins to brown. Drain on paper towels, reserving 1 tsp. drippings in skillet.

2. Add potatoes and onion to reserved drippings; sprinkle with rosemary and ¼ tsp. each of the salt and pepper. Cook over medium-high 5 to 6 minutes or until potatoes are light brown and onion is tender, turning occasionally.

3. Place pizza crust on a baking sheet;* brush with the 1 tsp. oil. Top with potato mixture and bacon. Bake about 10 minutes or until edge of crust is brown.

4. Meanwhile, for salad, remove 1 tsp. zest and squeeze 1 Tbsp. juice from lemon. In a medium bowl whisk together zest and juice, the 3 Tbsp. oil, the mustard, and the remaining ¼ tsp. each salt and pepper. Add arugula; toss to coat. Pile salad on top of pizza and sprinkle with cheese.

***Tip** For a crisper crust, bake the pizza directly on the oven rack.

EACH SERVING 314 cal., 18 g fat (4 g sat. fat), 11 mg chol., 525 mg sodium, 33 g carb., 4 g fiber, 4 g sugars, 9 g pro.

REUBEN BRAT SANDWICHES

MAKES 5 SERVINGS

5 cooked smoked bratwurst links

5 hoagie-style pretzel buns or bratwurst buns, split

5 slices Swiss cheese (6 oz. total), halved

1 recipe Quick Slaw

3 Tbsp. Thousand Island salad dressing

1. In a large grill pan or skillet cook bratwurst over medium 8 to 10 minutes or until heated through, turning occasionally.

2. Preheat broiler. Line a large baking sheet with foil. Split buns and fill with brats. Top brats with cheese. Broil 4 to 5 inches from heat 1 to 2 minutes or until cheese is melted.

3. Top with Quick Slaw. Drizzle with salad dressing.

Quick Slaw In a bowl combine 4 cups shredded cabbage and carrot (coleslaw mix); 1 medium yellow sweet pepper, cut into very thin bite-size strips (1¼ cups); 3 Tbsp. cider vinegar; 2 Tbsp. canola oil; 2 tsp. Dijon-style mustard; ½ tsp. caraway seeds, crushed; and ¼ tsp. each salt and black pepper. Toss to combine.

EACH SERVING 593 cal., 37 g fat (9 g sat. fat), 74 mg chol., 1,054 mg sodium, 8 g carb., 3 g fiber, 7 g sugars, 20 g pro.

ANDOUILLE CAULIFLOWER RICE SKILLET

SUPER QUICK	MAKES 4 SERVINGS

4 links cooked andouille sausage, bias-sliced (12 oz. total)

1 cup chopped red and/or yellow sweet pepper

½ cup chopped onion

½ cup sliced celery

1 Tbsp. vegetable oil

1 16-oz. pkg. cauliflower rice (4 cups)

1 5.2-oz. pkg. semisoft cheese with shallots and chives

¼ cup milk

1 tsp. Cajun seasoning

Chopped fresh parsley

1. In a large skillet cook sausage, sweet pepper, onion, and celery in oil over medium-high about 6 minutes or until vegetables are just tender and sausage is lightly browned, stirring frequently. Add cauliflower rice; cook and stir 2 minutes.

2. Add semisoft cheese, milk, and Cajun seasoning; stir until melted and smooth. Sprinkle with parsley.

EACH SERVING 397 cal., 30 g fat (15 g sat. fat), 89 mg chol., 880 mg sodium, 13 g carb., 3 g fiber, 6 g sugars, 21 g pro.

[MAKE A SWAP]

INSTEAD OF CAULIFLOWER RICE, YOU CAN USE 4 CUPS COOKED RICE. STIR IN RICE AT THE VERY END OF COOKING.

GREEK LAMB CHOP SKILLET

HEALTHY	MAKES 4 SERVINGS

8 lamb rib chops, cut
   1 inch thick

¼ tsp. salt

2 tsp. olive oil

1 lemon

½ cup chopped fresh parsley

2 Tbsp. chopped fresh
   oregano

8 cloves garlic, minced

1 15-oz. can butter beans
   or Great Northern beans,
   rinsed and drained

1 14.5-oz. can fire-roasted
   diced tomatoes, undrained

¼ to ½ tsp. coarsely ground
   black pepper

1. Trim fat from chops. Sprinkle chops with ⅛ tsp. of the salt. In a large skillet heat oil over medium. Add chops; cook about 8 minutes for medium (145°F), turning once. Remove chops from skillet, reserving drippings in skillet. Cover chops and keep warm.

2. Meanwhile, remove 1 tsp. zest and squeeze 1 to 2 Tbsp. juice from lemon. For gremolata, in a small bowl combine lemon zest, the remaining ⅛ tsp. salt, the parsley, 1 Tbsp. of the oregano, and two of the garlic cloves.

3. Stir the remaining 1 Tbsp. oregano and six garlic cloves, beans, and tomatoes into reserved drippings. Bring to boiling; reduce heat. Simmer, uncovered, 3 minutes. Stir in lemon juice. Serve chops on bean mixture and sprinkle with pepper and gremolata.

EACH SERVING 245 cal., 6 g fat (2 g sat. fat), 51 mg chol., 822 mg sodium, 23 g carb., 5 g fiber, 4 g sugars, 25 g pro.

PAN-GRILLED LAMB WITH PEACH SALSA

HEALTHY	MAKES 4 SERVINGS

3 medium fresh peaches, pitted and chopped (3 cups)

1 Tbsp. finely chopped fresh jalapeño chile pepper (tip, page 92)

4 tsp. red wine vinegar

1 Tbsp. honey

⅛ tsp. ground allspice

2 tsp. olive oil

¼ tsp. salt

⅛ tsp. cayenne pepper

8 lamb rib chops, cut ¾ to 1 inch thick

2 cups hot cooked multigrain rice blend

2 Tbsp. chopped roasted, salted pistachio nuts

1. For peach salsa, in a medium bowl combine peaches, jalapeño, 2 tsp. of the vinegar, the honey, and allspice. Stir gently to mix.

2. In a large bowl stir together olive oil, the remaining 2 tsp. vinegar, the salt, and cayenne pepper. Add lamb chops; toss to coat. In a large grill pan or skillet cook chops, in batches if necessary, over medium-high 6 to 8 minutes or until medium-rare (145°F), turning once.

3. Serve chops on rice blend with peach salsa. Top with pistachio nuts.

EACH SERVING 406 cal., 16 g fat (4 g sat. fat), 75 mg chol., 250 mg sodium, 39 g carb., 4 g fiber, 14 g sugars, 27 g pro.

[SPEED IT UP]

PICK UP A PACKAGE OF COOKED MULTIGRAIN BLEND. YOU'LL ONLY HAVE TO TEAR OPEN THE POUCH AND HEAT IT UP.

LAMB AND CUCUMBER SALAD PITAS

| MAKES 4 SERVINGS |

¼ cup lemon juice

3 Tbsp. olive oil

1 fresh jalapeño chile pepper, seeded and thinly sliced (tip, page 92)

1½ tsp. dried oregano, crushed

1 large cucumber, peeled, seeded, and coarsely chopped

1 cup thinly sliced red onion

½ cup pitted Kalamata olives, halved

½ cup packed fresh mint leaves

½ cup plain yogurt

1 clove garlic, minced
Salt and black pepper

1 lb. ground lamb

4 soft pita rounds, warmed

1. For cucumber salad, in a bowl combine lemon juice, 2 Tbsp. of the oil, the jalapeño, and oregano. Add cucumber, onion, olives, and half of the mint; toss to coat.

2. In a small bowl stir together yogurt and half of the garlic. Chop remaining mint and stir into yogurt mixture. Season to taste with salt and black pepper.

3. In a large bowl combine ground lamb, the remaining garlic, ½ tsp. salt, and ¼ tsp. black pepper. In an extra-large skillet heat the remaining 1 Tbsp. oil over medium-high. Using a slightly rounded ½-cup measure, spoon meat in four mounds into skillet. Cook 2 minutes. Press mounds into thin patties with the back of a wide spatula. Cook 4 to 5 minutes or until done (160°F), turning once.

4. Serve lamb patties on pitas topped with cucumber salad and yogurt mixture.

EACH SERVING 658 cal., 38 g fat (11 g sat. fat), 79 mg chol., 968 mg sodium, 48 g carb., 6 g fiber, 7 g sugars, 30 g pro.

HUMMUS AND LAMB PIZZA

MAKES 4 SERVINGS

- 8 oz. ground lamb, beef, or turkey
- ½ cup chopped onion
- 1 large clove garlic, minced
- 1 Tbsp. chopped fresh oregano
- ½ tsp. salt
- ½ tsp. freshly ground black pepper
- 1 12-inch packaged thin pizza crust
- 2 Tbsp. + 2 tsp. olive oil
- 1 10-oz. container hummus
- 2 Tbsp. cider vinegar
- 2 tsp. Dijon-style mustard
- 6 cups thinly sliced romaine lettuce
- 1 cup cherry tomatoes, halved
- ½ cup sliced sweet piquante, cherry, or Italian sweet peppers
- ½ cup crumbled feta cheese

1. Preheat oven to 450°F. In a large skillet cook ground lamb, onion, and garlic over medium-high until meat is browned. Drain off any fat. Stir in oregano, salt, and black pepper.

2. Place pizza crust on a large baking sheet;* brush with the 2 tsp. oil. Spread with hummus and top with lamb mixture. Bake 10 to 15 minutes or until edges of crust are lightly browned and crisp.

3. Meanwhile, for salad, in a large bowl whisk together the 2 Tbsp. oil, the vinegar, and mustard. Season to taste with additional salt and black pepper. Add lettuce, tomatoes, and piquante peppers; toss to coat. Pile salad on top of pizza and sprinkle with cheese.

*Tip For a crisper crust, bake the pizza directly on the oven rack.

EACH SERVING 631 cal., 32 g fat (9 g sat. fat), 50 mg chol., 942 mg sodium, 63 g carb., 5 g fiber, 4 g sugars, 22 g pro.

[MAKE A SWAP]

NAAN BREAD MAKES PERFECT PIZZA CRUST. USE TWO LARGE NAAN LOAVES IN PLACE OF THE SINGLE PIZZA CRUST

CHICKEN & TURKEY

THERE'S A REASON CHICKEN AND TURKEY OFTEN SHOW UP IN THE WEEKLY ROTATION—BONELESS CUTS AND PURCHASED ROASTED CHICKEN ARE QUICK TO PREPARE. FIND CREATIVE NEW TAKES ON POULTRY IN STIR-FRIES, CASSEROLES, PASTA TOSSES, SALADS, TACOS, AND MORE.

ROSEMARY CHICKEN AND GRITS

HEALTHY	MAKES 4 SERVINGS

4 skinless, boneless chicken breast halves (about 1½ lb. total)

1 Tbsp. chopped fresh rosemary

½ tsp. salt

¼ tsp. black pepper

1 Tbsp. olive oil

3 cups reduced-sodium chicken broth

1 cup quick-cooking (hominy) grits

2 cups red and/or green grapes, halved

½ cup chopped almonds

⅓ cup crumbled blue cheese or feta cheese

1. Sprinkle both sides of chicken with rosemary, salt, and pepper. In an extra-large nonstick skillet heat oil over medium-high. Add chicken; cook 10 to 12 minutes or until done (165°F), turning once.

2. Meanwhile, in a small saucepan bring broth to boiling; reduce heat to medium-low. Stir in grits. Cook 5 to 6 minutes or until thickened, stirring frequently.

3. Remove chicken from skillet. Add grapes and almonds to hot skillet. Cook and stir 2 to 3 minutes or until grapes are warm and nuts are lightly toasted. Serve chicken with grits and grape mixture. Sprinkle with cheese.

EACH SERVING 551 cal., 19 g fat (4 g sat. fat), 117 mg chol., 1,019 mg sodium, 49 g carb., 4 g fiber, 13 g sugars, 47 g pro.

LEMON-BRAISED CHICKEN TENDERS AND CAULIFLOWER

HEALTHY	MAKES 4 SERVINGS

1 large lemon
1 lb. chicken breast tenderloins
2 Tbsp. olive oil
2 cups cauliflower florets
⅓ cup chopped onion
5 cloves garlic, slivered
1 tsp. chopped fresh thyme
¼ tsp. salt
¼ tsp. cracked black pepper
¾ cup reduced-sodium chicken broth
4 cups baby spinach
¼ cup bias-sliced green onions
2 cups hot cooked brown rice (optional)
Fresh thyme sprigs (optional)

1. Remove 1 tsp. zest (more for garnish if desired) and squeeze ¼ cup juice from lemon. In an extra-large skillet cook chicken in hot oil over medium-high 6 to 8 minutes or until chicken is done (165°F), turning once. Remove from skillet; cover and keep warm.

2. Add cauliflower and chopped onion to skillet; cook about 2 minutes or until lightly browned, stirring frequently. Add garlic, snipped thyme, salt, and pepper; cook and stir 30 seconds more. Add lemon juice, stirring to scrape up the crusty browned bits. Add the 1 tsp. lemon zest and the broth. Bring to boiling; reduce heat. Simmer, covered, 6 to 8 minutes or until cauliflower is tender. Remove from heat.

3. Stir in chicken, spinach, and green onions. Cover and let stand about 2 minutes or until spinach is slightly wilted.

4. If desired, serve chicken mixture over brown rice and top with additional lemon zest and/or thyme sprigs.

EACH SERVING 235 cal., 10 g fat (2 g sat. fat), 73 mg chol., 442 mg sodium, 9 g carb., 3 g fiber, 2 g sugars, 28 g pro.

[MAKE A SWAP]

MAKE YOUR OWN CHICKEN BREAST TENDERS BY STARTING WITH SKINLESS, BONELESS CHICKEN BREASTS. CUT BREAST HALVES INTO ¾-INCH-WIDE STRIPS.

COCONUT CHICKEN WITH PINEAPPLE-MANGO SALSA

MAKES 4 SERVINGS

1 egg, lightly beaten
1 Tbsp. vegetable oil
½ tsp. salt
⅛ tsp. cayenne pepper
1¼ cups flaked coconut
14 to 16 oz. chicken breast tenderloins
1 8-oz. can pineapple tidbits (juice pack), drained
1 cup chopped refrigerated mango slices (about 10 slices)
2 Tbsp. chopped fresh cilantro (optional)
1 Tbsp. lime juice

1. Preheat oven to 400°F. Line a large baking sheet with foil; lightly grease foil.

2. In a shallow bowl whisk together egg, oil, ¼ tsp. of the salt, and the cayenne pepper. Spread coconut in a second shallow bowl. Dip each chicken piece in egg mixture, allowing excess to drip off. Coat chicken with coconut. Arrange chicken on the prepared baking sheet. Bake 10 to 12 minutes or until chicken is done (165°F).

3. Meanwhile, for salsa, in a bowl combine remaining ingredients and the remaining ¼ tsp. salt. Serve with chicken.

EACH SERVING 393 cal., 18 g fat (12 g sat. fat), 110 mg chol., 461 mg sodium, 31 g carb., 4 g fiber, 27 g sugars, 27 g pro.

CHICKEN TENDER KABOBS

HEALTHY	MAKES 4 SERVINGS

⅓ cup plain Greek yogurt

¼ cup light mayonnaise

2 Tbsp. water

1 tsp. sriracha sauce

½ tsp. salt

1 8-oz. pkg. whole fresh cremini or button mushrooms, stemmed

2 Tbsp. olive oil

2 Tbsp. red wine vinegar

1 tsp. dried oregano, crushed

1 tsp. ground cumin

¼ tsp. black pepper

8 chicken breast tenderloins (12 to 14 oz.)

8 miniature sweet peppers

1. For yogurt sauce, in a small bowl combine yogurt, mayonnaise, the water, sriracha sauce, and ¼ tsp. of the salt. Cover and chill until ready to serve.

2. In a large saucepan cook mushrooms in boiling water 1 minute; drain and pat dry. In a large bowl whisk together oil, vinegar, oregano, cumin, black pepper, and the remaining ¼ tsp. salt. Add mushrooms, chicken, and sweet peppers; toss to coat.

3. On four 12-inch skewers* alternately thread chicken (accordian-style), mushrooms, and sweet peppers. Grease grill rack. Grill chicken skewers, covered, over medium 10 to 12 minutes or until chicken is no longer pink (165°F), turning to brown evenly. Serve kabobs with yogurt sauce and, if desired, additional sriracha sauce.

***Tip** If using wooden skewers, soak in water 30 minutes; drain.

EACH SERVING 262 cal., 15 g fat (3 g sat. fat), 69 mg chol., 472 mg sodium, 9 g carb., 2 g fiber, 5 g sugars, 24 g pro.

[MAKE A SWAP]

ROSEMARY IS A CLASSIC MEDITERRANEAN HERB, BUT FOR A LESS-ASSERTIVE FLAVOR, TRY BASIL OR AN ITALIAN HERB BLEND.

KOREAN CHICKEN TACOS

HEALTHY	MAKES 4 SERVINGS

3 Tbsp. reduced-sodium soy sauce

1 Tbsp. lime juice

2 tsp. packed brown sugar

1½ tsp. grated fresh ginger

2 cloves garlic, minced

1 tsp. cornstarch

1 tsp. Asian chili-garlic sauce

1½ lb. skinless, boneless chicken breast halves, cut into bite-size strips

1 Tbsp. vegetable oil

1¼ cups kimchi

8 5- to 6-inch white corn tortillas, warmed

⅓ cup chopped fresh cilantro

Korean barbecue sauce (optional)

1. In a small bowl combine the first seven ingredients (through chili-garlic sauce).

2. In a large skillet cook and stir chicken in hot oil over medium 8 to 10 minutes or until no longer pink. Stir soy mixture; add to chicken in skillet. Cook and stir until thickened and bubbly.

3. Divide chicken mixture and kimchi among warm tortillas. Top with cilantro and, if desired, serve with barbecue sauce.

EACH SERVING 354 cal., 9 g fat (1 g sat. fat), 109 mg chol., 790 mg sodium, 26 g carb., 3 g fiber, 6 g sugars, 39 g pro.

[MAKE A SWAP]

NOT A KIMCHI FAN? USE A VINEGAR-BASED COLESLAW FROM THE SUPERMARKET DELI. IT JUST WON'T BE AS SPICY.

POTATO CHIP BAKED CHICKEN FINGERS

| SUPER QUICK | MAKES 4 SERVINGS |

3   Tbsp. vegetable oil
1   egg, lightly beaten
¼   cup sour cream
¼   tsp. salt
¼   tsp. garlic powder
¼   tsp. black pepper
1¼ to 1½ lb. chicken tenderloins
3   cups potato chips
1   recipe Saucy Pickle Dip

1. Preheat oven to 400°F. Brush a 15×10-inch baking pan with the oil. In a medium bowl whisk together the next five ingredients (through pepper). Add chicken, stirring to coat.

2. Place potato chips in a large resealable plastic bag; seal bag, pressing out air. Using a rolling pin, crush chips to make coarse crumbs. Transfer to a shallow dish. Add chicken strips, a few at a time, rolling and pressing to coat. Arrange chicken strips in the prepared baking pan, leaving space between each strip.

3. Bake 8 to 10 minutes or until chicken is no longer pink, turning after 5 minutes. Serve with Saucy Pickle Dip.

Saucy Pickle Dip In a small bowl stir together ½ cup ranch salad dressing, 3 Tbsp. ketchup, and 1 Tbsp. dill pickle relish.

EACH SERVING *505 cal., 29 g fat (5 g sat. fat), 148 mg chol., 1,053 mg sodium, 23 g carb., 1 g fiber, 2 g sugars, 35 g pro.*

CHICKEN, TOMATO, AND CUCUMBER SALAD

HEALTHY	SUPER QUICK	MAKES 4 SERVINGS

1 to 1¼ lb. chicken breast tenderloins
½ tsp. salt
½ tsp. black pepper
5 Tbsp. olive oil
¼ cup cider vinegar or white wine vinegar
1 Tbsp. chopped fresh thyme
1 tsp. sugar
1 medium cucumber, thinly sliced
2 tomatoes, sliced
1 cup crumbled feta cheese (4 oz.) (optional)
½ cup pitted green olives, halved and/or sliced

1. Sprinkle chicken with ¼ tsp. each of the salt and pepper. In a large skillet heat 1 Tbsp. of the oil over medium. Add chicken; cook 8 to 10 minutes or until no longer pink, turning once.

2. For vinaigrette, in a screw-top jar combine vinegar, thyme, sugar, the remaining 4 Tbsp. oil, and ¼ tsp. each salt and pepper. Cover and shake well.

3. Divide chicken; cucumber; tomatoes; cheese, if desired; and olives among plates. Drizzle with vinaigrette.

EACH SERVING 336 cal., 23 g fat (3 g sat. fat), 73 mg chol., 569 mg sodium, 7 g carb., 2 g fiber, 4 g sugars, 25 g pro.

[MAKE A SWAP]
SUBSTITUTE FISH FOR CHICKEN, ZUCCHINI OR CARROTS FOR CUCUMBERS, AND PITTED KALAMATA OR RIPE OLIVES FOR GREEN OLIVES.

MOROCCAN CHICKEN

HEALTHY	MAKES 6 SERVINGS

1 small orange
2 tsp. all-purpose flour
1½ tsp. ground turmeric
½ tsp. salt
½ tsp. ground cumin
½ tsp. ground coriander
⅛ tsp. cayenne pepper
1 lb. skinless, boneless chicken breast halves, cut into 1-inch pieces
2 Tbsp. olive oil
1 15-oz. can garbanzo beans (chickpeas), rinsed and drained
4 green onions, cut into ½-inch pieces
½ cup reduced-sodium chicken broth
¼ cup snipped dried apricots
1 tsp. grated fresh ginger
⅓ cup pitted green olives, halved
3 cups hot cooked jasmine or white rice

1. Using a vegetable peeler, remove two 1-inch-wide strips of peel from orange. Squeeze juice from orange. In a medium bowl stir together the next six ingredients (through cayenne pepper). Add chicken; toss gently to coat.

2. In a large skillet cook chicken and orange peel strips in hot oil over medium-high about 4 minutes or until chicken is no longer pink, stirring occasionally. Stir in the orange juice, garbanzo beans, half of the green onions, the broth, dried apricots, and ginger. Bring to boiling; reduce heat. Simmer, uncovered, 4 minutes. Stir in olives; cook and stir 1 minute more. Remove and discard orange peel strips.

3. Serve chicken mixture over hot cooked rice. Sprinkle with the remaining green onions.

EACH SERVING 368 cal., 10 g fat (1 g sat. fat), 48 mg chol., 614 mg sodium, 47 g carb., 2 g fiber, 5 g sugars, 24 g pro.

[**FINISH WITH FLAVOR**]

ADD A BRIGHT, CITRUSY NOTE BY SERVING CHICKEN WITH FRESH ORANGE WEDGES TO SQUEEZE OVER TOP.

PAN-FRIED CHICKEN WITH POLENTA AND VEGETABLES

HEALTHY	MAKES 4 SERVINGS

1 pint grape or cherry tomatoes

1 Tbsp. packed brown sugar

3 cups water

1½ tsp. salt

¾ cup quick-cooking polenta

⅓ cup all-purpose flour

½ tsp. salt

½ tsp. black pepper

½ cup buttermilk

2 8-oz. skinless, boneless chicken breast halves, halved horizontally

3 Tbsp. vegetable oil

1 9-oz. pkg. fresh spinach

1. Pierce tomatoes with a sharp knife. Place in a bowl; sprinkle with brown sugar. Cover loosely. Microwave about 3 minutes or until skins burst and tomatoes are soft, stirring once.

2. In a large saucepan bring the water and 1 tsp. of the salt to boiling; stir in polenta. Reduce heat; cook 5 minutes, stirring frequently.

3. In a shallow dish combine flour, the remaining ½ tsp. salt, and the pepper; pour buttermilk into another shallow dish. Dip chicken in buttermilk, then in flour, turning to coat. In an extra-large skillet heat oil over medium-high; add chicken. Cook 6 to 8 minutes or until no longer pink (165°F), turning to cook evenly. Remove chicken from skillet.

4. Discard pan drippings. Add spinach to hot skillet; cook and toss just until wilted. Season to taste with additional salt and pepper. Serve chicken with spinach, polenta, and tomato mixture.

EACH SERVING 506 cal., 14 g fat (2 g sat. fat), 75 mg chol., 483 mg sodium, 59 g carb., 8 g fiber, 7 g sugars, 33 g pro.

ASPARAGUS, CHICKEN, AND GREEN PEA SALAD

SUPER QUICK	MAKES 4 SERVINGS

1 cup water

1 lb. fresh asparagus spears, trimmed

1 cup fresh or frozen peas

2 cups shredded purchased roasted chicken

3 Tbsp. white balsamic vinegar

3 Tbsp. olive oil

½ tsp. salt

½ tsp. black pepper

⅛ tsp. crushed red pepper (optional)

1 cup crumbled goat cheese (chèvre) (4 oz.)

¼ cup torn fresh mint leaves

1. In a large skillet bring the water to boiling. Add asparagus. Return to boiling; reduce heat. Simmer, covered, 2 to 3 minutes or just until asparagus is crisp-tender. Place peas in colander. Pour water and asparagus over peas. Rinse with cold water; drain.

2. Arrange asparagus on a platter. Top with chicken and peas. For dressing, in a small bowl whisk together next five ingredients (through crushed red pepper). Drizzle salad with dressing and sprinkle with cheese and mint.

EACH SERVING 378 cal., 23 g fat (8 g sat. fat), 102 mg chol., 743 mg sodium, 13 g carb., 3 g fiber, 8 g sugars, 29 g pro.

[MAKE A SWAP]
TRADE THE MINT FOR 2 TABLESPOONS FRESH TARRAGON OR CHIVES.

SPICY PEANUT-CHICKEN NOODLES

HEALTHY	MAKES 6 SERVINGS

- 6 oz. pad thai-style brown rice noodles
- ¼ cup vegetable oil
- ¾ cup peanuts, coarsely chopped
- 1 fresh serrano chile pepper, thinly sliced (tip, page 92)
- 3 cups shredded purchased roasted chicken
- 2 cups packaged julienned carrots or coarsely shredded carrots
- ½ cup rice vinegar
- 2 Tbsp. fish sauce
- 2 tsp. sugar
- ¼ cup chopped fresh mint or Thai basil
- Lime wedges

1. Bring a large pot of water to boiling; turn off heat and add rice noodles. Let stand 5 to 6 minutes or until noodles are softened but not mushy; drain. Rinse with cold water; drain well. Transfer noodles to a large bowl.

2. In an extra-large skillet heat oil over medium. Add peanuts and chile pepper; cook about 5 minutes or until aromatic and chile slices are just beginning to brown, stirring frequently. Remove from heat; add shredded chicken and carrots, stirring until no longer sizzling.

3. In a small bowl combine rice vinegar, fish sauce, and sugar; pour over noodles. Add chicken mixture and mint; toss to coat. Serve immediately with lime wedges and, if desired, additional chopped fresh mint.

EACH SERVING 414 cal., 23 g fat (4 g sat. fat), 63 mg chol., 784 mg sodium, 31 g carb., 5 g fiber, 5 g sugars, 23 g pro.

To Make Ahead Prepare as directed. Chill up to 8 hours before serving.

ITALIAN CHICKEN ORZO SOUP

HEALTHY	MAKES 4 SERVINGS

2 14.5-oz. cans reduced-
   sodium chicken broth

1 lb. skinless, boneless chicken
   breast halves or thighs,
   cubed

1 14.5-oz. can diced tomatoes
   with basil, garlic, and
   oregano, undrained

½ cup dried orzo pasta

1 lemon

1 cup chopped zucchini or
   yellow summer squash

   Black pepper

4 to 6 Tbsp. basil pesto

1. In a large saucepan combine broth, chicken, tomatoes, and orzo. Bring to boiling; reduce heat. Simmer, uncovered, 6 minutes.

2. Meanwhile, remove 1 tsp. zest and squeeze 1 Tbsp. juice from lemon. Add zest, juice, and zucchini to soup. Return to boiling; reduce heat. Simmer, uncovered, 3 to 4 minutes or until orzo and zucchini are tender and chicken is no longer pink. Season to taste with pepper. Top servings with pesto.

EACH SERVING *371 cal., 12 g fat (0 g sat. fat), 68 mg chol., 1,180 mg sodium, 30 g carb., 1 g fiber, 8 g sugars, 35 g pro.*

[FINISH WITH FLAVOR]

INTENSIFY THE TOMATO FLAVOR BY USING SUN-DRIED TOMATO PESTO FOR ALL OR HALF OF THE BASIL PESTO.

CREAMY CHICKEN AND TOMATO PASTA

MAKES 4 SERVINGS

2½ cups dried campanelle pasta (8 oz.)

2 Tbsp. butter

¼ cup finely chopped onion

3 cloves garlic, minced

12 oz. fresh asparagus spears, trimmed and cut into 1-inch pieces

1 cup chopped seeded roma tomatoes

1 cup heavy cream

2 cups shredded purchased roasted chicken

⅓ grated Parmesan cheese

¼ cup shredded fresh basil

2 tsp. lemon zest

1. Cook pasta according to package directions. Drain, reserving ½ cup cooking water. Keep pasta warm.

2. Meanwhile, in a large skillet melt 1 Tbsp. of the butter over medium. Add onion and garlic; cook and stir 1 to 2 minutes or until tender. Add asparagus and tomatoes; cook and stir 1 minute. Add the reserved pasta cooking water, the cream, and the remaining 1 Tbsp. butter; cook and stir until butter is melted and liquid is slightly thickened. Stir in chicken and Parmesan; heat through. Add hot cooked pasta. Top with basil, lemon zest, and, if desired, additional grated Parmesan.

EACH SERVING 626 cal., 35 g fat (20 g sat. fat), 167 mg chol., 467 mg sodium, 50 g carb., 4 g fiber, 6 g sugars, 32 g pro.

[FINISH WITH FLAVOR]

BRINY CAPERS ADD DIMENSION TO PASTA DISHES. STIR IN 1 TABLESPOON DRAINED CAPERS WITH THE CHICKEN.

CHICKEN COBB WRAPS

MAKES 8 SERVINGS

4 10-inch flour tortillas
1 recipe Green Onion Aïoli
2 cups shredded purchased roasted chicken
2 cups thinly sliced leaf lettuce
8 slices bacon, crisp-cooked
2 hard-boiled eggs, sliced
1 avocado, halved, seeded, peeled, and sliced
¾ cup quartered grape tomatoes
½ cup crumbled blue cheese (2 oz.)

1. Spread each tortilla with 2 Tbsp. of the Green Onion Aïoli to within ½ inch of the edge. Layer bottom halves of tortillas with the remaining ingredients. Fold in sides and roll up tortillas. Cut tortillas in half. Serve with remaining aïoli for dipping.

Green Onion Aïoli In a small bowl combine 1 cup mayonnaise; 6 Tbsp. chopped green onions; 4 tsp. lemon juice; 2 cloves garlic, minced; and ½ tsp. cracked black pepper.

EACH SERVING 475 cal., 35 g fat (8 g sat. fat), 112 mg chol., 792 mg sodium, 22 g carb., 3 g fiber, 2 g sugars, 20 g pro.

SWEET AND SAVORY CHICKEN SALAD

1 fresh pineapple, peeled, cored, and cut lengthwise into 4 pieces

½ of a head napa cabbage, cut crosswise into 1-inch-thick pieces, or 2 hearts romaine lettuce, halved crosswise

1 2¼- to 2½-lb. purchased roasted chicken, meat removed from bones and cut into bite-size pieces (remove skin if desired)

1 cup green and/or red seedless grapes, halved

1 Granny Smith apple, sliced

½ cup ginger-sesame stir-fry sauce

¼ cup creamy peanut butter

¼ tsp. crushed red pepper

1. Slice pineapple pieces into ½-inch-thick slices. Arrange cabbage, chicken, grapes, apple slices, and pineapple on a platter or individual plates.

2. For dressing, in a small bowl whisk together stir-fry sauce, peanut butter, and crushed red pepper; if necessary, add water, 1 tsp. at a time, to reach drizzling consistency. Drizzle dressing over salad.

EACH SERVING 529 cal., 19 g fat (5 g sat. fat), 123 mg chol., 998 mg sodium, 44 g carb., 5 g fiber, 34 g sugars, 45 g pro.

QUICK CHICKEN PAELLA

MAKES 4 SERVINGS

8 oz. fresh or frozen medium shrimp

1 Tbsp. olive oil

4 oz. thinly sliced cooked smoked chorizo sausage links

1 cup chopped onion

2 cloves garlic, minced

1 14.5-oz. can diced tomatoes, undrained

1 14.5-oz. can chicken broth
Dash saffron threads

¾ cup Israeli couscous

2 cups shredded purchased roasted chicken

½ cup frozen peas
Chopped fresh parsley (optional)

1. Thaw shrimp if frozen. Peel and devein shrimp.

2. In an extra-large skillet heat oil over medium. Add chorizo, onion, and garlic; cook 5 minutes, stirring occasionally. Add tomatoes, broth, and saffron. Bring to boiling; stir in the couscous. Reduce heat. Cover and simmer 5 minutes.

3. Add shrimp, chicken, and peas to skillet; cover and cook about 5 minutes more or until shrimp are opaque and couscous is tender. If desired, top with parsley.

EACH SERVING 455 cal., 19 g fat (6 g sat. fat), 182 mg chol., 1,054 mg sodium, 32 g carb., 4 g fiber, 6 g sugars, 40 g pro.

PULLED CHICKEN AND TORTELLINI STEW

HEALTHY	MAKES 4 SERVINGS

10 to 12 oz. skinless, boneless chicken breast halves, cut into 2-inch pieces

1 14.5-oz. can fire-roasted diced tomatoes with garlic, undrained

1 14.5-oz. can reduced-sodium chicken broth

1 9-oz. pkg. refrigerated cheese-filled tortellini

2 cups bite-size pieces fresh asparagus

¼ cup dry white wine or strained cooking water from chicken

Quartered grape tomatoes, thinly sliced fresh basil, black pepper, and/or grated Parmesan cheese (optional)

1. In a 4-qt. Dutch oven cook chicken in enough water to cover 8 to 10 minutes or until no longer pink. Remove chicken. If desired, reserve and strain 1½ cups of the cooking water. Discard remaining water.

2. In Dutch oven bring canned tomatoes and chicken broth to boiling. Stir in tortellini; cook 3 minutes. Stir in asparagus; cook about 5 minutes more or just until tortellini and asparagus are tender.

3. Meanwhile, use two forks to shred chicken. Stir chicken and wine into tomato mixture. For a thinner soup, stir in desired amount of the strained chicken cooking water. If desired, top with grape tomatoes, basil, pepper, and/or Parmesan.

EACH SERVING 335 cal., 6 g fat (3 g sat. fat), 76 mg chol., 761 mg sodium, 38 g carb., 5 g fiber, 7 g sugars, 29 g pro.

[MAKE A SWAP]

YOU CAN SUBSTITUTE 3 CUPS CHOPPED FRESH SPINACH OR BABY KALE FOR THE ASPARAGUS. PREPARE AS DIRECTED, EXCEPT STIR IN THE GREENS WITH THE WINE AND HEAT JUST UNTIL GREENS ARE WILTED.

CHORI-POLLO BOLILLOS

MAKES 4 SERVINGS

8 oz. uncooked ground chorizo sausage

½ cup thinly sliced onion

3 cups shredded cooked chicken

1 8-oz. can tomato sauce

⅓ cup drained sliced pickled jalapeños

4 Mexican bolillo rolls or torta rolls, halved if large

1½ to 2 cups shredded chihuahua cheese or Monterey Jack cheese (6 to 8 oz.)

Chopped fresh cilantro (optional)

1. Preheat oven to 400°F. In a large skillet cook chorizo and onion over medium about 5 minutes or until chorizo is cooked and onion is tender, stirring occasionally. Stir in chicken, tomato sauce, and jalapeños. Cook 5 minutes to blend flavors, stirring occasionally.

2. Split rolls. Fill rolls with meat mixture and cheese. Arrange open sandwiches on a baking sheet. Bake 5 to 10 minutes or until toasted and cheese is melted. If desired, sprinkle with cilantro.

EACH SERVING 701 cal., 30 g fat (12 g sat. fat), 199 mg chol., 1,387 mg sodium, 49 g carb., 3 g fiber, 6 g sugars, 58 g pro.

[MAKE A SWAP]

MEXICAN BOLILLO ROLLS OR TORTA ROLLS ARE STURDY SPECIALTY ROLLS WITH A CHEWY TEXTURE. MEDIUM-SIZE CIABATTA ROLLS CAN BE USED INSTEAD.

GRANDE BURRITO BOWLS

MAKES 6 SERVINGS

2 to 3 Tbsp. vegetable oil

1 20-oz. pkg. refrigerated shredded Southwestern-style hash brown potatoes

½ of a ripe avocado, seeded and peeled

½ cup ranch salad dressing

½ tsp. ground cumin

1 15-oz. can black beans, rinsed and drained

1 cup frozen whole kernel corn, cooked according to package directions and cooled

2 Tbsp. lime juice

2 Tbsp. chopped fresh cilantro

6 cups mixed spring salad greens, baby kale, and/or chopped romaine lettuce

2 cups chopped smoked or plain cooked chicken

2 cups grape tomatoes, quartered

1. In an extra-large nonstick skillet with flared sides heat oil over medium. Add potatoes; press with the back of a spatula to form a cake. Cook, without stirring, about 10 minutes or until bottom is golden and crisp. Turn potato cake over, adding additional oil if needed.* Cook, without stirring, about 7 minutes more or until bottom is golden. Slide potato cake from skillet to a cutting board. Cut into six wedges.

2. Meanwhile, for dressing, in a small bowl mash avocado with a fork. Stir in ranch dressing and cumin.

3. In a medium bowl toss together beans, corn, lime juice, and 1 Tbsp. of the cilantro.

4. Arrange greens, chicken, tomatoes, and bean mixture in bowls. Add potato wedges. Drizzle with dressing and sprinkle with the remaining 1 Tbsp. cilantro.

*Tip To turn the potato cake, invert a baking sheet over top of skillet. Invert skillet with baking sheet to transfer potatoes to the sheet. If necessary, add additional oil to skillet. Using the baking sheet, slide potato cake back into skillet.

EACH SERVING 592 cal., 24 g fat (4 g sat. fat), 70 mg chol., 1,094 mg sodium, 65 g carb., 13 g fiber, 8 g sugars, 34 g pro.

[FINISH WITH FLAVOR]

BURRITO BOWLS ARE ULTRAFLEXIBLE. AS DESIRED, ADD FAVORITE INGREDIENTS, SUCH AS CHEESE, SHREDDED JICAMA, SLICED RIPE OLIVES, SALSA, AND HOT PEPPER SAUCE.

BLACKENED CHICKEN WITH SUCCOTASH

MAKES 4 SERVINGS

8 skinless, boneless chicken thighs (about 2¼ lb. total)

2 tsp. blackened seasoning

2 Tbsp. olive oil

2 strips bacon, chopped

1½ cups frozen roasted whole kernel corn

1 cup frozen shelled edamame

½ tsp. dried thyme, crushed

¾ cup cherry tomatoes, halved

¼ cup sliced green onions
Salt and black pepper

⅔ cup reduced-sodium chicken broth

2 Tbsp. heavy cream

2 Tbsp. butter

2 tsp. Dijon-style mustard

1. Sprinkle chicken all over with blackened seasoning. In an extra-large skillet heat oil over medium-high. Cook chicken 12 to 15 minutes or until chicken is done (170°F), turning chicken occasionally. Transfer to a platter; keep warm.

2. Meanwhile, for succotash, in a large skillet cook bacon over medium until crisp, stirring occasionally. Add corn, edamame, and thyme; cook and stir about 5 minutes or until crisp-tender. Stir in tomatoes, green onions, and salt and pepper to taste. Toss to combine and heat through. Add broth, stirring to loosen any browned bits. Bring to boiling; boil gently, uncovered, 3 to 5 minutes or until reduced by half. Add cream and butter, stirring until butter is melted. Stir in mustard. Return chicken to skillet; heat through.

Tip If you don't have two skillets, keep the chicken warm while preparing the succotash in the same skillet.

EACH SERVING 623 cal., 35 g fat (11 g sat. fat), 276 mg chol., 643 mg sodium, 17 g carb., 4 g fiber, 5 g sugars, 59 g pro.

QUICK CHICKEN PAPRIKASH

MAKES 6 SERVINGS

1¼ lb. skinless, boneless chicken thighs, cut into 1½-inch pieces

1 medium onion, cut into thin wedges

1 Tbsp. olive oil

1½ Tbsp. sweet paprika

½ tsp. salt

½ tsp. black pepper

1 14.5-oz. can diced tomatoes with basil, garlic, and oregano, undrained

1 cup reduced-sodium chicken broth

⅓ cup bottled sliced banana peppers

⅓ cup sour cream

2 Tbsp. all-purpose flour

4 cups hot cooked noodles

1. In a large skillet cook chicken and onion in hot oil over medium-high about 4 minutes or until chicken is starting to brown, stirring occasionally. Sprinkle with paprika, salt, and black pepper. Cook and stir 1 minute more.

2. Stir in tomatoes, broth, and banana peppers. Bring to boiling; reduce heat to medium-low. Cook, covered, 5 minutes. Increase heat to medium-high. Cook, uncovered, 4 to 6 minutes more or until mixture is slightly thickened, stirring frequently. In a small bowl stir together sour cream and flour; stir into chicken mixture. Cook and stir until thickened and bubbly.

3. Serve chicken mixture over hot cooked noodles. If desired, top with additional banana peppers.

EACH SERVING 300 cal., 10 g fat (3 g sat. fat), 117 mg chol., 650 mg sodium, 29 g carb., 2 g fiber, 4 g sugars, 24 g pro.

MOO SHU CHICKEN WRAPS

HEALTHY	INSTANT MEAL	MAKES 6 SERVINGS

½ cup hoisin sauce

2 Tbsp. water

4 tsp. toasted sesame oil

1 Tbsp. cornstarch

1 Tbsp. reduced-sodium soy sauce

3 large cloves garlic, minced

1 14- to 16-oz. pkg. shredded cabbage with carrots (coleslaw mix)

1 cup coarsely shredded carrots

12 oz. skinless, boneless chicken thighs, cut into ½-inch strips

6 8-inch flour tortillas, warmed

Sliced green onions

1. For sauce, in a small bowl combine the first six ingredients (through garlic).

2. In a 6-qt. multifunction electric or stove-top pressure cooker combine coleslaw mix, shredded carrots, and ¼ cup water. Place chicken on top of cabbage mixture. Drizzle with ¼ cup of the sauce. Lock lid in place. Set electric cooker on high pressure to cook 5 minutes. For a stove-top cooker, bring to pressure over medium-high heat; reduce heat enough to maintain steady (but not excessive) pressure. Cook 5 minutes. Remove from heat. For both models, let stand to release pressure naturally 15 minutes. Release any remaining pressure. Open lid carefully.

3. Using a slotted spoon, spoon chicken mixture down center of tortillas (discard cooking liquid). Drizzle with remaining sauce. Top with green onions.

EACH SERVING 321 cal., 10 g fat (2 g sat. fat), 54 mg chol., 874 mg sodium, 39 g carb., 4 g fiber, 10 g sugars, 14 g pro.

ASIAN-STYLE PULLED CHICKEN SLIDERS WITH SNOW PEA SLAW

HEALTHY	INSTANT MEAL	MAKES 6 SERVINGS

½ cup hoisin sauce

4 tsp. reduced-sodium soy sauce

4 tsp. minced fresh ginger

2 cloves garlic, minced

2 tsp. packed brown sugar

2 tsp. rice vinegar

1 lime

3 Tbsp. mayonnaise

1 tsp. sugar

6 oz. snow pea pods, halved crosswise, then cut lengthwise into thin strips

½ cup shredded carrot

2 green onions, thinly sliced

2 lb. skinless, boneless chicken thighs

1 large sweet onion, halved lengthwise and thinly sliced (1½ cups)

½ cup chicken broth

12 Slider buns, toasted

1. For the sauce, in a small bowl stir together the first six ingredients (through rice vinegar). For the slaw, remove 1 tsp. zest and squeeze 1 Tbsp. juice from lime. In a medium bowl stir together lime juice and zest, mayonnaise, and sugar. Add snow peas, carrot, and green onions; toss to coat. Cover and chill until ready to serve.

2. In a 3½- or 4-qt. multifunction electric or stove-top pressure cooker combine chicken and onion. Drizzle with chicken broth and ⅓ cup of the sauce. Lock lid in place. Set electric cooker on high pressure to cook 10 minutes. For stove-top cooker, bring up to pressure over medium-high heat; reduce heat enough to maintain steady (but not excessive) pressure. Cook 10 minutes. Remove from heat. For both models, let stand 15 minutes to release pressure naturally. Release any remaining pressure.

3. Using a slotted spoon, transfer chicken and onions to a bowl; discard cooking liquid. Using two forks, shred chicken. Add the remaining sauce to the bowl; toss to coat. Serve chicken mixture on buns with slaw.

EACH SERVING 503 cal., 16 g fat (3 g sat. fat), 148 mg chol., 1,003 mg sodium, 50 g carb., 4 g fiber, 15 g sugars, 38 g pro.

[SPEED IT UP]

SKIP SOME OF THE PREP. A PURCHASED CREAMY COLESLAW CAN BE USED INSTEAD OF MAKING THE SNOW PEA SLAW IN STEP 1.

CHICKEN GYRO BOWLS

INSTANT MEAL	MAKES 4 SERVINGS

1¼ lb. skinless, boneless chicken thighs

1 tsp. Greek seasoning

1 cup chopped onion

½ cup red wine vinaigrette salad dressing

¼ cup water

2 cloves garlic, minced

2 cups shredded romaine lettuce

1 cup halved grape or cherry tomatoes

1 cup tzatziki sauce

1 cup pita chips

Crumbled feta cheese, Kalamata olives, and/or chopped red onion

1. Sprinkle chicken with Greek seasoning. In a 6-qt. multifunction electric or stove-top pressure cooker combine chicken and the next four ingredients (through garlic).

2. Lock lid in place. Set electric cooker on high pressure to cook 5 minutes. For stove-top cooker, bring up to pressure over medium-high heat; reduce heat enough to maintain steady (but not excessive) pressure. Cook 5 minutes. Remove from heat. For both models, let stand 15 minutes to release pressure naturally. Release any remaining pressure. Open lid carefully. Transfer chicken to a bowl. Using two forks, shred chicken. Use a slotted spoon to remove onion from cooker to bowl with chicken; stir to combine.

3. In bowls arrange shredded chicken mixture, lettuce, tomatoes, tzatziki sauce, and pita chips. Top with feta, Kalamata olives, and/or red onion.

EACH SERVING 488 cal., 27 g fat (11 g sat. fat), 141 mg chol., 999 mg sodium, 29 g carb., 2 g fiber, 11 g sugars, 34 g pro.

[MAKE A SWAP]

CAN'T FIND PREPARED TZATZIKI SAUCE? STIR TOGETHER 1 CUP CHOPPED CUCUMBER; ⅔ CUP PLAIN GREEK YOGURT; 1 CLOVE GARLIC, MINCED; AND ¼ TEASPOON SALT.

CHICKEN MEATBALL NOODLE BOWL

HEALTHY	MAKES 4 SERVINGS

 4 oz. dried thin rice noodles or angel hair pasta
12 oz. ground chicken
 2 Tbsp. chopped fresh cilantro (optional)
 1 Tbsp. grated fresh ginger or 1 tsp. ground ginger
 ½ tsp. salt
 3 Tbsp. canola oil
 1 medium red Fresno chile pepper, seeded and finely chopped (tip, page 92) (optional)
 ⅓ cup rice vinegar
 2 Tbsp. honey
 1 Tbsp. lime juice
 3 cups shredded leaf lettuce
 ½ cup finely shredded carrot
    Sliced green onions (optional)
    Lime wedges (optional)

1. Prepare noodles according to package directions; drain.

2. Meanwhile, in a large bowl combine ground chicken, cilantro, the ginger, and salt. Shape mixture into 16 meatballs. In a large skillet heat 1 Tbsp. of the oil over medium. Add meatballs; cook about 10 minutes or until done (165°F),* turning to brown evenly. Remove meatballs from skillet. Turn off heat.

3. Add the remaining 2 Tbsp. oil and, if desired, the chopped chile pepper to the still-warm skillet. Stir in rice vinegar, honey, and lime juice.

4. Divide noodles, lettuce, and carrot among bowls. Top with meatballs; drizzle with vinegar mixture. If desired, top with additional cilantro and sliced chile pepper and/or green onions and serve with lime wedges.

*Tip The internal color of a meatball is not a reliable doneness indicator. A chicken meatball cooked to 165°F is safe, regardless of color. To measure the doneness of a meatball, insert an instant-read thermometer into the center of the meatball.

EACH SERVING 369 cal., 17 g fat (3 g sat. fat), 73 mg chol., 413 mg sodium, 36 g carb., 1 g fiber, 10 g sugars, 16 g pro.

SPICY CHICKEN SAUSAGE PASTA AND GREENS

HEALTHY	MAKES 4 SERVINGS

3 cups dried medium shell macaroni (8 oz.)

1 bunch Broccolini, trimmed and cut into 1-inch pieces (3 cups)

1 12-oz. pkg. cooked spicy chicken sausage links, cut into ½-inch slices

⅓ cup coarsely chopped onion

3 cloves garlic, minced

2 Tbsp. olive oil

1 cup reduced-sodium chicken broth

½ tsp. kosher salt

¼ tsp. black pepper

1 to 2 cups arugula

¼ cup chopped fresh dill

¼ cup grated Parmesan cheese

Crushed red pepper (optional)

1. In a 4-qt. Dutch oven cook pasta according to package directions, adding Broccolini the last 4 minutes of cooking; drain. Rinse with cold water; drain again.

2. In an extra-large skillet cook sausage, onion, and garlic in hot oil over medium-high about 3 minutes or until sausage is browned, turning occasionally. Stir in pasta mixture, broth, salt, and black pepper; heat through. Remove from heat. Add arugula and dill; toss gently until greens are wilted.

3. Divide pasta mixture among shallow bowls. Sprinkle with cheese. If desired, drizzle with a little additional olive oil and sprinkle with crushed red pepper.

EACH SERVING 432 cal., 13 g fat (4 g sat. fat), 69 mg chol., 847 mg sodium, 52 g carb., 4 g fiber, 5 g sugars, 28 g pro.

[MAKE A SWAP]

BROCCOLINI, WHICH LOOKS LIKE SLENDER STALKS OF BROCCOLI, IS NOT ALWAYS AVAILABLE. YOU CAN USE SMALL BROCCOLI FLORETS OR CUT LARGE FLORETS INTO LONG STRIPS.

FENNEL, GRAPEFRUIT, AND TURKEY SALAD

MAKES 6 SERVINGS

¼ cup finely chopped shallots

2 Tbsp. white wine vinegar

½ tsp. kosher salt

¼ tsp. black pepper

½ cup olive oil

¼ cup sour cream

2 Tbsp. finely chopped fresh tarragon

½ cup pine nuts

8 cups butterhead (Boston or Bibb) lettuce

1 cup thinly sliced seedless cucumber

1 small fennel bulb, trimmed, cored, and cut into thin wedges

2 medium pink grapefruit, peeled and cut into ¼-inch slices

1 cup crumbled feta cheese (4 oz.)

8 oz. smoked turkey breast

1. For dressing, in a small bowl combine shallots, vinegar, salt, and pepper. Whisk in 7 Tbsp. of the oil, the sour cream, and tarragon.

2. In a medium skillet cook pine nuts and the remaining 1 Tbsp. oil over medium 3 to 5 minutes or until nuts are toasted, stirring occasionally. Sprinkle with additional salt.

3. In a large bowl combine lettuce, cucumber, and fennel. Drizzle with dressing; toss to coat. Add grapefruit and cheese; toss gently to combine. Top with smoked turkey and pine nuts.

EACH SERVING 403 cal., 33 g fat (7 g sat. fat), 37 mg chol., 637 mg sodium, 18 g carb., 4 g fiber, 10 g sugars, 14 g pro.

[MAKE A SWAP]

GIVE THIS SALAD SOME BITE BY USING MUSTARD GREENS OR ARUGULA FOR SOME OR ALL OF THE BUTTERHEAD LETTUCE.

GARLIC-LEMON TURKEY AND ASPARAGUS

HEALTHY	INSTANT MEAL	MAKES 6 SERVINGS

2 turkey breast tenderloins
   (1½ to 1¾ lb. total)

¼ tsp. salt

¼ tsp. black pepper

1 Tbsp. olive oil

½ cup chicken broth

1 lemon, sliced

10 to 12 cloves garlic, peeled
    and coarsely chopped

2 sprigs fresh thyme

1½ lb. fresh asparagus spears,
    trimmed and steamed

2 Tbsp. Dijon-style mustard

2 Tbsp. sour cream

1. Sprinkle turkey breast tenderloins with the salt and pepper. In a 6-qt. multifunction electric cooker or stove-top pressure cooker cook turkey in hot oil about 4 minutes or until browned, turning once. (For an electric cooker, use sauté setting.) Add broth, lemon, garlic, and thyme to cooker.

2. Lock lid in place. Set electric cooker on high pressure to cook 15 minutes. For stove-top cooker, bring up to pressure over medium-high heat; reduce heat enough to maintain steady (but not excessive) pressure. Cook 15 minutes. Remove from heat. For both models, release pressure quickly. Open lid carefully.

3. Transfer turkey to cutting board; slice crosswise. Place on serving platter with steamed asparagus and additional lemon slices; cover to keep warm. Strain liquid from cooker. Measure ¼ cup liquid; whisk in mustard and sour cream. Pass sauce with turkey and asparagus. Season to taste with additional salt and pepper.

EACH SERVING 154 cal., 4 g fat (1 g sat. fat), 73 mg chol., 255 mg sodium, 2 g carb., 1 g fiber, 1 g sugars, 29 g pro.

[SPEED IT UP]

STEAM THE ASPARAGUS WHILE THE TURKEY COOKS.

TURKEY-POMEGRANATE STIR-FRY

HEALTHY	SUPER QUICK	MAKES 4 SERVINGS

1 tsp. ground cumin

½ tsp. ground coriander

½ tsp. paprika

1 lb. turkey breast tenderloins, cut into 1-inch pieces

1 Tbsp. olive oil

1 cup thinly bias-sliced carrots or parsnips

1 medium onion, cut into wedges

¼ cup pomegranate seeds

2 cups hot cooked couscous (optional)

Chopped pistachio nuts

1. In a medium bowl stir together cumin, coriander, and paprika. Add turkey; toss to coat. In a wok or extra-large skillet heat oil over medium-high. Add carrots and onion; cook and stir 2 minutes. Add turkey; cook and stir 5 minutes. Add pomegranate seeds. Cook and stir 1 to 2 minutes more or until turkey is no longer pink and vegetables are tender, adding enough water to reach desired sauciness.

2. If desired, serve turkey mixture over couscous. Top with pistachios and/or additional pomegranate seeds.

EACH SERVING 216 cal., 7 g fat (1 g sat. fat), 51 mg chol., 117 mg sodium, 10 g carb., 3 g fiber, 5 g sugars, 28 g pro.

[SPEED IT UP]

LOOK FOR CONTAINERS OF FRESH POMEGRANATE SEEDS (ALSO KNOWN AS ARILS) IN THE REFRIGERATED SECTION OF THE PRODUCE DEPARTMENT RATHER THAN SEEDING A WHOLE POMEGRANATE.

TURKEY-CUCUMBER SANDWICHES WITH CITRUS-CILANTRO SPREAD

MAKES 4 SERVINGS

1 lemon
1 cup plain fat-free Greek yogurt
½ cup chopped fresh cilantro
½ cup reduced-fat feta cheese
½ tsp. ground cumin
4 whole grain naan bread
2 cups lightly packed baby spinach
1 lb. cooked turkey breast, thinly sliced
2 cups cucumber ribbons*
⅔ cup thin slivers red onion

1. Remove ½ tsp. zest and squeeze 4 tsp. juice from lemon. In a bowl stir together zest and juice, and the next four ingredients (through cumin).

2. Top naan halves with spinach leaves. Carefully spread yogurt mixture over spinach. Top with turkey, cucumber, and onion. Roll up naan.

*Tip Use a vegetable peeler to cut cucumber lengthwise into thin ribbons.

EACH SERVING 612 cal., 16 g fat (6 g sat. fat), 100 mg chol., 1,142 mg sodium, 66 g carb., 10 g fiber, 1 g sugars, 54 g pro.

TOMATO-BASIL TURKEY BURGERS

MAKES 8 SERVINGS

2 lb. ground turkey

2 Tbsp. chopped fresh basil

2 to 3 Tbsp. finely chopped oil-packed dried tomatoes

1 tsp. salt

½ tsp. black pepper
   Nonstick cooking spray

4 whole grain rolls or hamburger buns, split and toasted

1 yellow sweet pepper, roasted and cut into strips,* or ¾ cup bottled roasted red sweet pepper strips (optional)

1 recipe Bruschetta Topping or purchased fresh bruschetta topping

2 cups lightly packed arugula (optional)

1. In a large bowl combine the first five ingredients (through black pepper); mix well. Shape mixture into eight ½-inch-thick patties.

2. Coat a grill pan with cooking spray; heat over medium. Add patties to hot pan; cook 10 to 13 minutes or until done (165°F), turning once.

3. Serve burgers on roll halves with roasted pepper (if using), Bruschetta Topping, and, if desired, arugula.

*Tip To roast a sweet pepper in a grill pan, quarter pepper lengthwise; remove stem, seeds, and membranes. Cook pepper quarters, skin sides down, over medium about 10 minutes or until charred and very tender. Wrap pepper in foil; let stand 15 minutes or until cool enough to handle. Peel off and discard skin. Cut pepper into strips.

Bruschetta Topping In a small bowl combine ½ cup each chopped tomato and halved mozzarella pearls, ¼ cup chopped red onion, and 2 Tbsp. each chopped fresh parsley and basil. Drizzle with 2 Tbsp. olive oil; season to taste with salt and black pepper.

EACH SERVING 282 cal., 15 g fat (4 g sat. fat), 89 mg chol., 543 mg sodium, 11 g carb., 1 g fiber, 3 g sugars, 25 g pro.

SPICY STIR-FRIED TURKEY AND GREENS

MAKES 4 SERVINGS

2 medium red sweet peppers, seeded and cut into 1-inch pieces

1 small onion, cut into ½-inch-thick wedges

1 Tbsp. canola oil

2 cloves garlic, minced

1 lb. ground turkey

2 to 3 tsp. curry powder

1 1-inch piece fresh ginger, grated

½ tsp. salt

½ tsp. black pepper

6 cups fresh spinach

2 to 4 Tbsp. water

1 6-oz. carton plain low-fat yogurt

4 cups hot cooked couscous
Sliced almonds, toasted (optional)

1. In a large skillet or wok cook and stir sweet peppers and onion in hot oil over medium-high 3 minutes. Add garlic; cook and stir 1 minute more. Remove from skillet.

2. Add ground turkey, curry powder, ginger, salt, and pepper to hot skillet. Cook and stir about 5 minutes or until turkey is no longer pink. Add spinach and the water; return vegetables to skillet. Cook and stir just until spinach is wilted. Stir in yogurt. Serve turkey mixture over hot cooked couscous. If desired, sprinkle with almonds.

EACH SERVING 479 cal., 19 g fat (5 g sat. fat), 91 mg chol., 426 mg sodium, 48 g carb., 5 g fiber, 6 g sugars, 29 g pro.

SKILLET TACO PIE

MAKES 6 SERVINGS

1 lb. ground turkey breast or extra-lean ground beef

1 fresh poblano chile pepper, seeded and chopped (tip, page 92)

1 15-oz. can no-salt-added black beans, rinsed and drained

1 8-oz. can tomato sauce

½ cup salsa

1 tsp. chili powder

½ tsp. ground cumin

4 taco shells, broken

¼ cup sliced green onions

1 cup shredded reduced-fat cheddar cheese or Mexican-style four-cheese blend (4 oz.)

Shredded lettuce and chopped fresh tomatoes

1. In a large skillet cook turkey and poblano pepper over medium-high until meat is browned. Stir in the next five ingredients (through cumin). Bring to boiling; reduce heat to medium. Simmer, covered, about 5 minutes or until slightly thickened. Stir in half of the broken taco shells and the green onions.

2. Top turkey mixture with remaining broken taco shells, the cheese, lettuce, and tomatoes.

EACH SERVING 242 cal., 7 g fat (3 g sat. fat), 60 mg chol., 574 mg sodium, 20 g carb., 5 g fiber, 3 g sugars, 29 g pro.

[FINISH IT WITH FLAVOR]

TOP THIS SPOONABLE PIE WITH ANY FAVORITE NACHO TOPPINGS: SALSA, PICKLED JALAPEÑOS, SLICED RIPE OLIVES, HOT PEPPER SAUCE, GUACAMOLE, SOUR CREAM, OR FRESH CILANTRO.

POPPIN' TOMATO AND SAUSAGE SPAGHETTI SAUCE

HEALTHY	MAKES 6 SERVINGS

12 oz. bulk spicy turkey sausage

4 cloves garlic, smashed

2 10-oz. pkg. grape tomatoes

1 cup water

2 Tbsp. tomato paste

⅓ cup torn fresh basil leaves

2 Tbsp. olive oil

1 Tbsp. honey

¼ tsp. salt

¼ tsp. black pepper

6 cups hot cooked pasta
Grated Parmesan cheese (optional)

1. In an extra-large skillet cook sausage and garlic over medium-high 6 to 7 minutes or until sausage is browned. Stir in tomatoes. Cook 10 to 12 minutes more or until tomatoes begin to break down, stirring frequently. Stir in the water and tomato paste.

2. Bring to boiling; reduce heat. Simmer, uncovered, about 3 minutes or until slightly thickened. Stir in basil, oil, honey, salt, and pepper; heat through. Serve over pasta and, if desired, sprinkle with cheese and additional basil.

EACH SERVING 380 cal., 11 g fat (2 g sat. fat), 31 mg chol., 497 mg sodium, 52 g carb., 4 g fiber, 7 g sugars, 18 g pro.

FISH & SHELLFISH

FISH COOKS IN A FLASH—JUST WHAT YOU NEED TO GET DINNER ON THE TABLE FAST! PLUS, IT'S NUTRITIOUS AND LEAN. WE'LL SHOW YOU HOW TO ACCENT THE FLAVORS OF YOUR FAVORITE FISH AND SHELLFISH WITH THE RIGHT SEASONINGS, SAUCES, AND TOPPINGS.

ARCTIC CHAR WITH GREEN OLIVE AND LEMON DRESSING

MAKES 4 SERVINGS

4 5-oz. fresh or frozen arctic char fillets with skin, ½ to ¾ inch thick

1 lemon

½ cup green olives, rinsed, pitted,* and coarsely chopped

1 Tbsp. capers, rinsed and drained

4 Tbsp. olive oil
   Coarse salt and freshly ground black pepper

½ cup loosely packed fresh Italian parsley, coarsely chopped

1. Thaw fish if frozen. Remove zest and squeeze juice from lemon. For dressing, in a small saucepan combine zest and juice, olives, and capers. Slowly stir in 3 Tbsp. of the oil until combined. Heat dressing over low 5 to 10 minutes or until warm, stirring occasionally (do not simmer).

2. Preheat broiler. Line a baking pan with foil. Rinse fish; pat dry. Sprinkle fish with salt and pepper. Lightly rub both sides with the remaining 1 Tbsp. oil. Place, skin sides down, in prepared pan. Broil 4 to 5 inches from heat about 7 minutes or until fish flakes easily.

3. Before serving, stir parsley into dressing. Serve fish with dressing.

*Tip To pit olives, place on a cutting board and crush, one at a time, with the side of a chef's knife. Pull olive pieces away from the pit.

EACH SERVING 354 cal., 25 g fat (4 g sat. fat), 78 mg chol., 473 mg sodium, 2 g carb., 1 g fiber, 1 g sugars, 29 g pro.

[MAKE A SWAP]

SALMON IS AN EXCELLENT OPTION IF YOU CAN'T FIND ARCTIC CHAR.

FISH WITH CRISPY BREAD CRUMBS, KALE, AND ONIONS

MAKES 4 SERVINGS

4   5- to 6-oz. fresh or frozen skinless flounder, sole, tilapia, or cod fillets, ½ inch thick
    Kosher salt and freshly ground black pepper
2   lemons
1   cup coarse soft bread crumbs
1   Tbsp. chopped fresh tarragon
4   Tbsp. butter
1   Tbsp. olive oil
4   cups halved and sliced sweet onions (1¼ lb.)
1   5- to 6-oz. pkg. fresh baby kale

1. Thaw fish if frozen. Sprinkle with salt and pepper. Slice one of the lemons; halve the remaining lemon.

2. In a small bowl combine bread crumbs, tarragon, and dash salt. In an extra-large skillet heat 1 Tbsp. of the butter over medium. Add crumb mixture; cook and stir 4 to 5 minutes or until toasted. Remove from skillet.

3. In same skillet heat 2 Tbsp. of the butter and the oil over medium. Add onions and dash salt; cook 5 minutes. Add lemon slices. Cook about 5 minutes more or until onions are tender, stirring occasionally. Add kale; toss until lightly wilted. Remove from skillet.

4. In same skillet heat the remaining 1 Tbsp. butter over medium. Add fish; cook 4 to 6 minutes or until fish flakes easily, turning once. Top fish with crumb mixture. Serve with kale mixture and lemon halves.

EACH SERVING 396 cal., 18 g fat (8 g sat. fat), 112 mg chol., 436 mg sodium, 25 g carb., 5 g fiber, 8 g sugars, 36 g pro.

LEMON AND DILL FISH PACKETS

HEALTHY	INSTANT MEAL	MAKES 2 SERVINGS

2 5- to 6-oz. fresh or frozen tilapia or cod fillets
¼ tsp. salt
¼ tsp. garlic powder
¼ tsp. black pepper
2 sprigs fresh dill
4 slices lemon
2 tsp. butter
1 cup water

1. Thaw fish if frozen. Place each fillet in the center of a large square of parchment paper. Sprinkle fish with salt, garlic powder, and pepper; add dill. Top with lemon and butter. Bring up two opposite edges of paper; seal with a double fold. Fold remaining ends to enclose fish, leaving space for steam to build.

2. Place a steam rack in the bottom of a 6-qt. multifunction electric pressure cooker or stove-top pressure cooker; add the water. Place fish packets on rack.

3. Lock lid in place. Set electric cooker on high pressure to cook 5 minutes. For stove-top cooker, bring up to pressure over medium-high heat; reduce heat enough to maintain steady (but not excessive) pressure. Cook 5 minutes. Remove from heat. For both models, release pressure quickly. Open lid carefully. Let stand 5 minutes before serving.

EACH SERVING 162 cal., 6 g fat (3 g sat. fat), 10 mg chol., 396 mg sodium, 3 g carb., 1 g fiber, 1 g sugars, 26 g pro.

[MAKE A SWAP]

SEE HOW EASILY YOU CAN CHANGE THE FLAVOR OF THIS SIMPLE DISH BY USING FRESH BASIL, TARRAGON, OREGANO, CHIVES, THYME, OR PARSLEY FOR THE DILL.

OPEN-FACE FLOUNDER SANDWICH

HEALTHY	MAKES 4 SERVINGS

1 lemon, halved

⅓ cup mayonnaise

2 Tbsp. finely chopped shallot

1 Tbsp. pickle relish

1 tsp. Dijon-style mustard
Freshly ground black pepper

1½ lb. fresh flounder or other firm white fish fillets
Salt

2 Tbsp. all-purpose flour

3 Tbsp. vegetable oil

4 slices sourdough bread, toasted

4 cups mixed herbs and greens, such as parsley, chives, basil, cilantro, spinach, and/or sorrel, coarsely chopped

1. Squeeze juice from half of the lemon; cut remaining half into wedges. For sauce, in a small bowl combine lemon juice, mayonnaise, shallot, relish, and mustard. Season to taste with pepper.

2. Cut fish into four portions; sprinkle lightly with salt. Sprinkle flour on a plate. Dip fish in flour, turning to coat. In a large skillet heat oil over medium-high. Add fish (do not crowd; cook in batches if needed). Cook 4 to 6 minutes per ½-inch thickness or until fish flakes easily, turning once.

3. Spread sauce over bread slices; sprinkle with half of the herbs and greens. Top with fish and the remaining herbs and greens. Serve with lemon wedges.

EACH SERVING 555 cal., 29 g fat (4 g sat. fat), 89 mg chol., 841 mg sodium, 39 g carb., 4 g fiber, 4 g sugars, 37 g pro.

GOLDEN TURMERIC FISH

MAKES 4 SERVINGS

4 5- to 6-oz. fresh or frozen red snapper fish fillets, skin on
2 Tbsp. unrefined coconut oil*
2 Tbsp. fresh lime juice
1 Tbsp. grated fresh ginger
1 tsp. ground coriander
½ tsp. ground turmeric
⅛ tsp. cayenne pepper
½ tsp. salt
¼ tsp. freshly ground black pepper
   Chopped fresh cilantro
   Lime wedges

1. Thaw fish if frozen. Preheat broiler. Grease a broiler pan. Place fillets skin sides down on pan. In a small bowl combine the first six ingredients (through cayenne pepper). Season fillets with salt and black pepper. Spread coconut oil mixture over fillets.

2. Broil fillets 4 to 5 inches from heat 8 to 10 minutes or until fish flakes easily. Top with cilantro and lime wedges.

*Tip Coconut oil is solid at room temperature, just like shortening, and turns liquid when it is warm. It does not matter whether it is solid or liquid when you stir it with the spices.

EACH SERVING 268 cal., 9 g fat (6 g sat. fat), 52 mg chol., 382 mg sodium, 16 g carb., 0 g fiber, 9 g sugars, 29 g pro.

[FINISH WITH FLAVOR]

MANGO CHUTNEY PAIRS PERFECTLY WITH THE WARM SPICES OF THIS FISH DISH.

STEAMED TILAPIA WITH ASPARAGUS AND ORANGES

HEALTHY	MAKES 4 SERVINGS

- 2 oranges
- 2 cups reduced-sodium chicken broth
- ½ tsp. grated fresh ginger
- 1 lb. fresh asparagus spears, trimmed and halved
- 4 4- to 6-oz. fresh tilapia, orange roughy, or cod fillets
- 2 Tbsp. reduced-sodium soy sauce or coconut aminos
- 1 cup couscous
- 1 Tbsp. chopped fresh chives or dill (optional)

1. Remove ½ tsp. zest and squeeze ¼ cup juice from one of the oranges. Peel and section the remaining orange.

2. In an extra-large deep skillet combine orange juice, broth, and ginger. Place a large steamer basket in skillet. Bring to boiling. Add asparagus to basket; reduce heat to medium. Steam, covered, about 4 minutes or until asparagus is crisp-tender. Remove asparagus; cover and keep warm.

3. Add fish to basket in skillet. Pour soy sauce over fish. Steam, covered, 4 to 6 minutes per ½-inch thickness or just until fish flakes. Remove from heat. Remove fish; cover and keep warm.

4. Stir couscous and orange zest into broth mixture in skillet. Let stand, covered, 5 minutes. Fluff with a fork.

5. Serve fish and asparagus with couscous. Top with orange sections and, if desired, sprinkle with chives.

EACH SERVING 333 cal., 2 g fat (1 g sat. fat), 57 mg chol., 617 mg sodium, 45 g carb., 4 g fiber, 7 g sugars, 33 g pro.

[MAKE A SWAP]

IF TANGERINES OR CARA CARA ORANGES ARE IN SEASON, USE THEM INSTEAD OF REGULAR ORANGES.

HALIBUT AND ARUGULA WITH CHARRED GREEN ONION VINAIGRETTE

HEALTHY	MAKES 4 SERVINGS

4 4- to 6-oz. fresh halibut or cod fillets, ¾ to 1 inch thick
2 whole green onions
¼ cup olive oil
2 tsp. dried fines herbes or Italian seasoning, crushed
   Salt and black pepper
1 lemon
1 Tbsp. honey
1 tsp. dried oregano, crushed
1 clove garlic, minced
4 cups baby arugula
1 to 2 watermelon radishes* or 3 or 4 red radishes, thinly sliced

1. Drizzle fish and green onions with 1½ tsp. of the oil and sprinkle with fines herbes; rub over fish and onions. Heat grill pan over medium-high. Add fish and green onions to hot pan, half at a time if needed. Cook until fish flakes easily and onions are lightly charred, turning once. (Allow 4 to 6 minutes per ½-inch thickness of fish and 4 minutes for onions.) Season fish to taste with salt and pepper. Finely chop green onions.

2. For vinaigrette, remove 1 tsp. zest and squeeze 2 Tbsp. juice from lemon. In a small bowl combine zest and juice, green onions, honey, oregano, and garlic. Whisk in the remaining 3½ Tbsp. oil.

3. In a large bowl combine arugula and radishes. Drizzle with half of the vinaigrette; toss to coat. Divide arugula mixture among plates. Top with fish and drizzle with the remaining vinaigrette. If desired, serve with additional lemon.

*Tip With a light green or white exterior and a vibrant pink interior, a watermelon radish resembles a watermelon when sliced. It adds crunch to salads and a peppery-sweet flavor.

EACH SERVING 252 cal., 15 g fat (2 g sat. fat), 55 mg chol., 232 mg sodium, 7 g carb., 1 g fiber, 5 g sugars, 22 g pro.

PAN-GRILLED MAHI MAHI WITH AVOCADO SAUCE

HEALTHY	SUPER QUICK	MAKES 4 SERVINGS

4   6-oz. fresh or frozen
    mahi mahi or halibut fillets

½   of an 8-oz. pkg.
    refrigerated guacamole

⅓   cup buttermilk

1   Tbsp. prepared horseradish

½   tsp. Dijon-style mustard

¼   tsp. chili powder (optional)

1   Tbsp. olive oil

1   tsp. chili powder

¼   tsp. salt

¼   tsp. black pepper
    Nonstick cooking spray

2   Tbsp. lemon or lime juice

1   5-oz. pkg. baby spinach,
    wilted (optional)

1. Thaw fish if frozen. For sauce, in a small bowl stir together guacamole, buttermilk, horseradish, and mustard. If desired, sprinkle with the ¼ tsp. chili powder.

2. Brush fish with oil and sprinkle with the 1 tsp. chili powder, the salt, and pepper. Coat a grill pan with cooking spray; heat over medium. Add fish; cook 4 to 6 minutes per ½-inch thickness or until fish flakes easily, turning once. Drizzle with lemon juice.

3. Serve fish with sauce and, if desired, wilted spinach.

EACH SERVING 248 cal., 10 g fat (2 g sat. fat), 125 mg chol., 450 mg sodium, 5 g carb., 2 g fiber, 2 g sugars, 33 g pro.

ASIAN TUNA BOWLS

HEALTHY	SUPER QUICK	MAKES 4 SERVINGS

3 Tbsp. rice vinegar

2 Tbsp. reduced-sodium soy sauce

1 Tbsp. honey

1 tsp. toasted sesame oil

1 Tbsp. vegetable oil

12 oz. fresh tuna steaks, ¾ inch thick

1⅓ cups hot cooked rice

1 English cucumber, sliced

1 medium avocado, halved, seeded, peeled, and sliced

1⅓ cups microgreens or mixed greens

4 green onions, thinly bias-sliced (optional)

Lime wedges (optional)

1. For sauce, in a small bowl whisk together the first four ingredients (through sesame oil).

2. In a large skillet heat the vegetable oil over medium-high. Add the tuna steaks and cook 4 to 6 minutes or until slightly pink in center, turning once. Thinly slice.

3. Divide rice among four bowls. Top with tuna, cucumber, avocado, and microgreens. Serve with sauce and, if desired, green onions and/or lime wedges.

EACH SERVING 296 cal., 11 g fat (1 g sat. fat), 38 mg chol., 279 mg sodium, 28 g carb., 4 g fiber, 7 g sugars, 23 g pro.

[SPEED IT UP]

HIGH-QUALITY CANNED TUNA MAKES A FAST AND ECONOMICAL SUBSTITUTE FOR FRESH TUNA STEAKS. SKIP THE COOKING.

NIÇOISE SALAD SANDWICHES

SUPER QUICK	MAKES 4 SERVINGS

½ cup fresh thin green beans, trimmed

4 leaves butterhead (Boston or Bibb) lettuce

4 whole wheat or plain pita bread rounds

2 5-oz. cans solid light tuna packed in oil, drained

1 medium tomato, thinly sliced

½ of a medium red onion, thinly sliced

2 hard-boiled eggs, sliced (optional)

1 recipe Fresh Parsley Gremolata Vinaigrette or purchased Greek vinaigrette

1. Steam green beans or cook in boiling water 4 to 5 minutes or just until crisp-tender. Plunge into ice water; drain. Place a lettuce leaf on each pita round. Arrange green beans on lettuce. Top with tuna, tomato, red onion, and, if desired, egg slices. Drizzle with Fresh Parsley Gremolata Vinaigrette. Fold over to serve.

Fresh Parsley Gremolata Vinaigrette In a screw-top jar combine ¼ cup white wine vinegar; ¼ cup olive oil; 2 Tbsp. chopped fresh parsley; 2 tsp. Dijon-style mustard; 2 cloves garlic, minced; ½ tsp. lemon zest; and ¼ tsp. each salt and cracked black pepper. Cover and shake well to combine.

EACH SERVING 411 cal., 19 g fat (3 g sat. fat), 9 mg chol., 752 mg sodium, 40 g carb., 5 g fiber, 4 g sugars, 22 g pro.

LEMON-ROASTED TUNA AND ASPARAGUS

HEALTHY	SUPER QUICK	MAKES 4 SERVINGS

3 lemons

¼ cup olive oil

½ tsp. freshly ground black pepper

¼ tsp. salt

4 4-oz. fresh tuna steaks, cut ¾ inch thick

12 oz. fresh asparagus spears, trimmed

1 5-oz. pkg. mixed baby salad greens

⅓ cup shaved Parmesan cheese (optional)

1. Preheat oven to 450°F. Remove 2 tsp. zest and squeeze 3 Tbsp. juice from two of the lemons. Cut remaining lemon into wedges. For dressing, in a small bowl whisk together lemon zest and juice, oil, pepper, and salt.

2. In a 15×10-inch baking pan arrange tuna and asparagus. Brush with 2 to 3 Tbsp. of the dressing. Roast 6 to 8 minutes or just until tuna flakes easily and asparagus is crisp-tender.

3. In a large bowl drizzle salad greens with the remaining dressing; toss to coat. If desired, sprinkle tuna and asparagus with cheese. Serve with salad greens and lemon wedges.

EACH SERVING 310 cal., 19 g fat (3 g sat. fat), 43 mg chol., 198 mg sodium, 9 g carb., 4 g fiber, 2 g sugars, 29 g pro.

SALMON WITH LENTIL HASH AND BACON

HEALTHY	INSTANT MEAL	MAKES 4 SERVINGS

2 cups reduced-sodium chicken broth

1 lb. baby yellow potatoes, quartered

1 small head cauliflower (1½ lb.), cut into large florets

1 cup brown lentils, rinsed and drained

1 large onion, cut into quarters

4 cloves garlic, minced

1 Tbsp. curry powder

¼ to ½ tsp. kosher salt

½ tsp. ground cumin

½ tsp. ground coriander

¼ tsp. cayenne pepper

1 1½-lb. salmon fillet, skinned
  Black pepper

4 slices bacon, crisp-cooked, drained, and crumbled
  Fresh mint leaves

1. In a 6-qt. multifunction electric or stove-top pressure cooker stir together the first 11 ingredients (through cayenne). Cut salmon fillet in half crosswise; season with additional salt and black pepper. Place salmon on top of vegetables in cooker.

2. Lock the lid in place. Set electric cooker on high pressure to cook 1 minute. For a stove-top cooker, bring up to pressure over medium-high heat; remove from heat (no cook time). For both models, release pressure quickly. Open lid carefully. Top servings with crumbled bacon and fresh mint.

EACH SERVING 582 cal., 15 g fat (3 g sat. fat), 101 mg chol., 600 mg sodium, 59 g carb., 11 g fiber, 6 g sugars, 54 g pro.

SALMON WITH TOMATOES AND OLIVES

HEALTHY	MAKES 4 SERVINGS

2 small oranges

4 4-oz. fresh or frozen skinless salmon fillets

Salt and black pepper

1 Tbsp. olive oil

¼ cup sliced shallots

2 cloves garlic, minced

2 cups red and/or yellow grape or cherry tomatoes, halved if large

½ cup halved pitted Kalamata olives

Small fresh oregano leaves

1. Using a vegetable peeler, remove the zest from one of the oranges in strips. Cut the second orange into wedges.

2. Thaw salmon if frozen. Season with salt and pepper. In an extra-large nonstick skillet heat oil over medium-high. Add salmon; cook 6 to 8 minutes or until fish flakes easily, turning once. Remove fish from skillet; cover to keep warm.

3. In the same skillet cook shallots and garlic over medium 2 to 3 minutes or until tender. Add tomatoes; cook 2 to 3 minutes or until tomatoes soften and begin to release their juice. Stir in olives and orange zest strips.

4. Return salmon to skillet. Sprinkle with fresh oregano and serve.

EACH SERVING 257 cal., 13 g fat (2 g sat. fat), 62 mg chol., 316 mg sodium, 11 g carb., 3 g fiber, 5 g sugars, 24 g pro.

SPINACH AND SRIRACHA SALMON CAKES

MAKES 4 SERVINGS

- 1 lb. fresh or frozen skinless salmon fillets
- 2 cups spinach leaves
- ¾ cup soft bread crumbs
- 1 egg white
- 4 tsp. sriracha sauce
- ¼ tsp. salt
- 2 cups cooked wheat berries
- 2 Tbsp. vegetable oil
- 2 Tbsp. butter
- 1 lemon, halved

1. Thaw salmon if frozen. Cut half of the salmon into large pieces. Chop the remaining salmon into ½-inch pieces. Coarsely chop 1 cup of the spinach.

2. In a food processor combine large pieces of salmon, chopped spinach, bread crumbs, egg white, 2 tsp. of the sriracha sauce, and the salt. Cover and process until mixed. Transfer to a medium bowl; stir in chopped salmon (mixture will be soft). Shape into four ¾-inch-thick cakes.

3. In a large skillet heat oil over medium. Add salmon cakes; cook 10 to 12 minutes or until done (160°F), turning once. Add remaining spinach to skillet; cook and stir 1 to 2 minutes or until wilted. Stir spinach into wheat berries. Divide among plates and top with salmon cakes.

4. Drain oil from skillet. Melt butter in hot skillet; remove from heat. Add the remaining 2 tsp. sriracha sauce and squeeze juice from half of the lemon into skillet; stir to combine. Drizzle mixture over salmon cakes and spinach. Cut remaining lemon half into wedges and serve with salmon cakes.

EACH SERVING 470 cal., 21 g fat (6 g sat. fat), 77 mg chol., 445 mg sodium, 40 g carb., 7 g fiber, 2 g sugars, 32 g pro.

[MAKE A SWAP]

WHEAT BERRIES ARE JUST ONE WHOLE GRAIN YOU CAN ENJOY WITH THESE SALMON CAKES. TRY FARRO, BARLEY, BROWN RICE, WILD RICE, OR A MULTIGRAIN BLEND.

PEPPERED SALMON WITH ROASTED ROOT VEGETABLES

| HEALTHY | MAKES 4 SERVINGS |

- 4 4- to 5-oz. fresh or frozen skinless salmon fillets
- 2 cups coarsely chopped carrots
- 1 cup peeled and coarsely chopped red and/or golden beets
- 3 Tbsp. olive oil
- ¾ tsp. salt
- ¾ tsp. coarsely ground black pepper
- 2 large oranges
    Chopped green onions (optional)

1. Thaw salmon if frozen. Preheat oven to 425°F. Line a 13x9-inch baking pan with foil. Arrange carrots and beets in separate halves of the prepared pan. Drizzle with half of the olive oil and sprinkle with ½ tsp. each of the salt and pepper. Roast 20 to 25 minutes or until tender, stirring once. Transfer to a platter; cover to keep warm.

2. Meanwhile, remove 1 tsp. zest and squeeze ½ cup juice from one of the oranges. Cut remaining orange into slices. Sprinkle with the remaining ¼ tsp. each salt and pepper. In an extra-large skillet heat the remaining olive oil over medium-high. Add salmon; cook 4 to 6 minutes per ½-inch thickness or until salmon flakes easily, turning once. Transfer to platter with vegetables.

3. Add orange zest and juice to skillet. Simmer, uncovered, 3 to 5 minutes or until reduced by half; spoon over salmon. Serve orange slices with salmon. If desired, sprinkle with green onions.

EACH SERVING 323 cal., 18 g fat (3 g sat. fat), 62 mg chol., 534 mg sodium, 17 g carb., 4 g fiber, 11 g sugars, 24 g pro.

GRILLED SALMON AND LEEKS WITH ROSEMARY-MUSTARD BUTTER

MAKES 4 SERVINGS

1½ lb. leeks

2 Tbsp. olive oil

½ tsp. salt

½ tsp. black pepper

1 fresh rosemary sprig

4 4- to 6-oz. fresh salmon fillets with skin, ¾ to 1 inch thick

¼ cup unsalted butter, softened

2 tsp. Dijon-style mustard

1. Trim dark green tops and root ends from leeks, leaving ends intact. Cut leeks in half lengthwise; peel off tough outer leaves. Rinse leeks; pat dry. (Keep some water on leeks to prevent burning on the grill.) Brush leeks with 1 Tbsp. of the oil; sprinkle with ¼ tsp. each of the salt and pepper.

2. Grill rosemary sprig, uncovered, over medium-high 1 to 2 minutes or until lightly charred; remove. Grill leeks, covered, 5 to 7 minutes or until tender, turning occasionally. Remove; cover to keep warm.

3. Brush salmon with the remaining 1 Tbsp. oil and sprinkle with the remaining ¼ tsp. each salt and pepper. Add salmon, skin sides up, to grill. Grill, covered, 4 minutes. Turn and grill, covered, about 2 minutes more or until fish flakes easily. Remove from grill.

4. Strip rosemary leaves from stem; chop 1 tsp. leaves. In a small bowl stir together butter, mustard, and chopped rosemary leaves. Spread salmon and leeks with butter mixture and sprinkle with remaining rosemary leaves.

EACH SERVING 369 cal., 26 g fat (9 g sat. fat), 93 mg chol., 415 mg sodium, 11 g carb., 1 g fiber, 3 g sugars, 24 g pro.

COLD LOX NOODLE BOWL

HEALTHY	MAKES 4 SERVINGS

8 oz. dried spaghetti

¼ cup olive oil

¼ cup lime juice

1 Tbsp. grated fresh ginger

¼ tsp. salt

4 cups thinly sliced romaine heart

1 cup very thinly sliced radishes

1 fresh jalapeño chile pepper, thinly sliced (tip, p. 92)

¼ cup thinly sliced green onions

8 oz. thinly sliced smoked lox-style salmon

Crushed red pepper (optional)

1. Cook pasta according to package directions. Drain and rinse under cold water. Drain well.

2. Meanwhile, for dressing, in a small bowl whisk together the next four ingredients (through salt).

3. Divide spaghetti, romaine, radishes, jalapeño, and green onions among bowls. Top with lox and drizzle with dressing. If desired, sprinkle with crushed red pepper.

EACH SERVING 413 cal., 16 g fat (2 g sat. fat), 25 mg chol., 731 mg sodium, 48 g carb., 4 g fiber, 3 g sugars, 21 g pro.

[SPEED IT UP]

CUT THE PASTA COOKING TIME IN HALF BY USING SUPER-THIN ANGEL HAIR PASTA (ALSO KNOWN AS VERMICELLI OR CAPELLINI) INSTEAD OF SPAGHETTI.

WARM SHRIMP AND BABY POTATO SALAD

HEALTHY	MAKES 4 SERVINGS

1 lb. baby yellow potatoes

6 oz. trimmed whole green beans

¼ cup cider vinegar

1 Tbsp. Dijon-style mustard

2 cloves garlic, minced

½ tsp. salt

½ tsp. black pepper

¼ cup olive oil

1 lb. frozen peeled and deveined cooked large shrimp, thawed

4 cups mixed spring greens

½ cup fresh dill fronds

1. In a 4- to 5-qt. Dutch oven cook potatoes in a large amount of boiling water 10 minutes. Add beans; return to boiling. Cook about 4 minutes more or until potatoes are tender; drain.

2. Meanwhile, in an extra-large bowl whisk together the next five ingredients (through pepper). Gradually whisk in oil until combined. Add potato mixture and shrimp; toss to coat. In a medium bowl toss greens with half of the dill.

3. Serve warm potato mixture over greens mixture. Sprinkle with the remaining dill.

Tip If you prefer a chilled salad, cook and drain the potatoes and beans as directed, except rinse with cold water and drain again.

EACH SERVING 326 cal., 14 g fat (2 g sat. fat), 183 mg chol., 621 mg sodium, 23 g carb., 5 g fiber, 3 g sugars, 26 g pro.

[MAKE A SWAP]

COOKED CHICKEN AND CANNED TUNA ARE GOOD OPTIONS FOR THE SHRIMP IN THIS FRENCH-STYLE SALAD.

CHILE-LIME HALIBUT WITH CORN SAUTÉ

HEALTHY	MAKES 4 SERVINGS

4 4- to 5-oz. fresh or frozen skinless halibut, sole, or tilapia fillets

1 Tbsp. lime juice

1 tsp. ground ancho chile pepper or chili powder

¼ tsp. salt

3 tsp. canola oil

2⅔ cups frozen whole kernel corn, thawed

¼ cup finely chopped red onion

2 tsp. finely chopped, seeded fresh jalapeño chile pepper (tip, p. 92)

1 clove garlic, minced

1 Tbsp. chopped fresh cilantro

Lime wedges (optional)

1. Thaw fish if frozen. In a small bowl combine lime juice, ground ancho pepper, and salt. Brush both sides of fish with lime mixture.

2. In a large nonstick skillet heat 2 tsp. of the oil over medium-high. Add fish; cook 4 to 6 minutes per ½-inch thickness or until fish flakes easily, turning once. Remove fish from skillet; cover and keep warm.

3. In same skillet heat remaining 1 tsp. oil over medium-high. Add corn, onion, jalapeño pepper, and garlic. Cook about 2 minutes or until vegetables are heated through and just starting to soften, stirring occasionally. Remove from heat. Stir in cilantro.

4. Serve fish with corn mixture and, if desired, lime wedges.

EACH SERVING 288 cal., 13 g fat (2 g sat. fat), 53 mg chol., 216 mg sodium, 25 g carb., 3 g fiber, 3 g sugars, 21 g pro.

SPICY SHRIMP FRIED CAULIFLOWER RICE

HEALTHY	MAKES 4 SERVINGS

8   oz. fresh or frozen medium shrimp in shells, peeled and deveined

1   1¾- to 2-lb. head cauliflower, broken into florets (4½ cups)

1   tsp. toasted sesame oil

2   eggs, lightly beaten

1   Tbsp. olive oil

4   tsp. grated fresh ginger

4   cloves garlic, minced

2   cups coarsely chopped napa cabbage

1   cup coarsely shredded carrots

½   tsp. sea salt

½   tsp. crushed red pepper

⅓   cup sliced green onions

2   Tbsp. chopped fresh cilantro
     Lime wedges

1. Thaw shrimp if frozen. Working in batches, place cauliflower in a food processor; cover and pulse until chopped into rice-size pieces.

2. In a wok or extra-large skillet heat sesame oil over medium. Add egg mixture; stir gently until set. Remove egg; cool slightly. Cut egg into strips.

3. In wok heat olive oil over medium-high. Add ginger and garlic; cook and stir 30 seconds. Add cabbage and carrots; cook and stir about 2 minutes or until vegetables start to soften. Add cauliflower; cook and stir about 4 minutes or until cauliflower starts to soften. Add shrimp, salt, and crushed red pepper; cook and stir about 2 minutes or until shrimp are opaque. Add cooked egg and green onions; cook and stir until heated.

4. Sprinkle shrimp mixture with cilantro. Serve with lime wedges.

EACH SERVING 181 cal., 8 g fat (2 g sat. fat), 172 mg chol., 434 mg sodium, 14 g carb., 5 g fiber, 5 g sugars, 17 g pro.

[SPEED IT UP]

START WITH PURCHASED RICED CAULIFLOWER FROM THE PRODUCE SECTION OF YOUR SUPERMARKET AND SKIP MAKING YOUR OWN IN STEP 1. YOU CAN ALSO USE RICED BROCCOLI FOR HALF OF THE AMOUNT.

SHRIMP SALAD WITH LIME DRESSING

HEALTHY	MAKES 4 SERVINGS

1 large lime
½ tsp. kosher salt
¼ tsp. cayenne pepper
2 Tbsp. olive oil
1 lb. fresh large shrimp in shells
1 tsp. olive oil
2 avocados, halved, seeded, peeled, and sliced
1 large tomato, cut into chunks
1 cup thinly sliced sweet onion
½ cup packed fresh cilantro leaves

1. If using wooden skewers, soak in water 30 minutes. For dressing, remove 1 tsp. zest and squeeze 3 Tbsp. juice from lime. In a small bowl combine zest and juice, ¼ tsp. of the salt, and the cayenne pepper. Slowly whisk in the 2 Tbsp. oil until combined.

2. Peel and devein shrimp, leaving tails intact if desired. In a bowl combine shrimp, the 1 tsp. oil, and the remaining ¼ tsp. salt; toss to coat. Thread shrimp onto skewers, leaving ¼ inch between shrimp. Grease grill rack. Grill shrimp skewers, covered, over medium 3 to 4 minutes or until shrimp are opaque, turning once.

3. On a large platter arrange shrimp, avocados, tomato, and onion. Drizzle with dressing and sprinkle with cilantro.

EACH SERVING 291 cal., 19 g fat (3 g sat. fat), 159 mg chol., 373 mg sodium, 12 g carb., 6 g fiber, 3 g sugars, 22 g pro.

TERIYAKI-GLAZED SHRIMP AND NOODLE STIR-FRY

HEALTHY	MAKES 4 SERVINGS

1 lb. fresh or frozen medium shrimp in shells

12 green onions

1 Tbsp. toasted sesame oil

1 Tbsp. grated fresh ginger

2 cups sugar snap pea pods, trimmed

1 14.2-oz. pkg. cooked udon noodles*

1 cup fresh pineapple chunks

3 Tbsp. reduced-sodium teriyaki sauce

3 Tbsp. water

¼ cup unsalted dry-roasted peanuts

1. Thaw shrimp if frozen. Peel and devein shrimp, leaving tails intact if desired. Chop 1 Tbsp. of the dark green tops of onions for garnish. Cut pale green and white parts into 2-inch pieces.

2. In a wok or extra-large skillet heat oil over medium-high. Add ginger; cook and stir 30 seconds. Add green onion pieces and snap peas; cook and stir 1 to 2 minutes. Add shrimp, noodles, and pineapple; cook and stir just until shrimp are opaque. Add teriyaki sauce and the water; toss to coat. Sprinkle with peanuts and green onion tops.

*Tip To help prevent the noodles from breaking apart, soften them in the microwave about 1 minute before using.

EACH SERVING 390 cal., 10 g fat (1 g sat. fat), 159 mg chol., 530 mg sodium, 47 g carb., 5 g fiber, 10 g sugars, 30 g pro.

SEARED SHRIMP AND BROCCOLI BOWLS

HEALTHY	MAKES 4 SERVINGS

1¼ lb. fresh or frozen large shrimp in shells

2 tsp. chili powder

¼ tsp. salt

6 tsp. canola oil

4 cups broccoli florets

½ cup red sweet pepper strips

4 Tbsp. water

1 lime

2 Tbsp. tahini (sesame seed paste)

2 cloves garlic, minced

¼ tsp. crushed red pepper

⅛ tsp. salt

1 8.8-oz. pouch cooked whole grain brown rice, heated according to package directions

1. Thaw shrimp if frozen. Peel and devein shrimp, leaving tails intact if desired. Sprinkle with chili powder and the ¼ tsp. salt. In an extra-large skillet heat 2 tsp. of the oil over medium-high. Add shrimp; cook about 4 minutes or until opaque, turning once. Remove from skillet; cover and keep warm.

2. In the skillet combine broccoli, sweet pepper, and 2 Tbsp. of the water. Cook, covered, over medium about 6 minutes or until broccoli is crisp-tender and browned, stirring occasionally.

3. Meanwhile, for dressing, remove ¼ tsp. zest and squeeze 2 Tbsp. juice from the lime. In a small bowl whisk together zest and juice, the remaining 4 tsp. of the oil and 2 Tbsp. water, and the next four ingredients (through ⅛ tsp. salt).

4. Divide shrimp, vegetables, and rice among bowls. Drizzle bowls with dressing.

EACH SERVING 354 cal., 13 g fat (1 g sat. fat), 228 mg chol., 465 mg sodium, 28 g carb., 5 g fiber, 3 g sugars, 35 g pro.

[FINISH WITH FLAVOR]

TOP BOWLS WITH FRESH CILANTRO AND ADD WEDGES OF LIME FOR AN EXTRA SQUEEZE OF TARTNESS.

SHRIMP PASTA DIAVOLO

HEALTHY	SUPER QUICK	MAKES 4 SERVINGS

1 9-oz. pkg. refrigerated linguine

1 medium onion, cut into thin wedges

3 cloves garlic, minced

¼ tsp. crushed red pepper

2 Tbsp. olive oil

1 14.5-oz. can diced tomatoes, undrained

1 8-oz. can tomato sauce

12 oz. medium fresh shrimp, peeled and deveined

2 cups baby spinach

½ cup torn fresh basil

½ cup finely shredded Parmesan cheese (2 oz.)

1. In a large saucepan cook pasta according to package directions. Drain pasta and return to pan.

2. Meanwhile, in a large skillet cook onion, garlic, and crushed red pepper in hot oil over medium until tender. Stir in tomatoes and tomato sauce. Bring to boiling; reduce heat. Simmer, uncovered, 3 minutes. Add shrimp to skillet; cover and simmer about 3 minutes or until shrimp are opaque. Add shrimp mixture to pasta. Stir in spinach and basil. Top with Parmesan cheese.

EACH SERVING *390 cal., 12 g fat (4 g sat. fat), 177 mg chol., 759 mg sodium, 45 g carb., 4 g fiber, 7 g sugars, 27 g pro.*

SPINACH, SCALLOP, AND QUINOA SALAD

HEALTHY	MAKES 6 SERVINGS

2 Tbsp. vegetable or canola oil

12 oz. fresh sea scallops

4 cups baby spinach

1½ cups cooked quinoa

1 cup torn radicchio

2 medium oranges, peeled, seeded, and sliced

½ of a medium red onion, cut into slivers

½ cup dried cranberries

1 recipe Orange-Poppy Seed Dressing

1. In a large skillet heat oil over medium-high. Add scallops; cook about 4 minutes or until browned and opaque, turning once.

2. In a large bowl combine scallops and the next six ingredients (through cranberries). Drizzle with Orange-Poppy Seed Dressing; toss to coat.

Orange-Poppy Seed Dressing Remove 1½ tsp. zest from 1 medium orange. Peel, seed, and section orange, reserving juice. In a food processor or blender combine orange zest, sections, and juice; 3 Tbsp. sherry vinegar or cider vinegar; 2 Tbsp. each sugar and Dijon-style mustard; 1 Tbsp. finely chopped onion; and dash black pepper. Cover and process or blend until nearly smooth. With processor or blender running, slowly add ⅓ cup canola oil in a steady stream until mixture is thickened. Transfer to a small bowl. Stir in 1 tsp. poppy seeds. Store in refrigerator up to 1 week. Stir before using. Makes about 1 cup.

EACH SERVING 357 cal., 18 g fat (1 g sat. fat), 23 mg chol., 464 mg sodium, 36 g carb., 4 g fiber, 19 g sugars, 15 g pro.

SCALLOPS AND PEACHES WITH PASTA

HEALTHY	MAKES 4 SERVINGS

- 2 cups dried gemelli or penne pasta (6 oz.)
- 1 lb. fresh or frozen bay scallops or 12 oz. peeled and deveined medium shrimp
- ⅓ cup olive oil
- ⅓ cup champagne vinegar
- ⅓ cup minced shallots or onion
- 2 tsp. lemon zest
- 2 cups chopped fresh peaches or nectarines (3)

  Salt and black pepper
- 4 cups arugula or baby spinach and arugula mix

  Parmesan cheese shavings (optional)

1. Cook pasta according to package directions, adding scallops the last 3 minutes of cooking; drain. Quickly rinse with cold water to cool; drain well.

2. Meanwhile, in a large bowl whisk together the olive oil, vinegar, shallots, and lemon zest. Add pasta and scallop mixture and the peaches; gently toss. Season to taste with salt and pepper. Add arugula; toss to combine. If desired, top with Parmesan shavings.

EACH SERVING 495 cal., 20 g fat (3 g sat. fat), 27 mg chol., 602 mg sodium, 56 g carb., 4 g fiber, 10 g sugars, 23 g pro.

[MAKE A SWAP]

IF FRESH PEACH AND NECTARINE SEASON HAS PASSED, SUBSTITUTE CHOPPED ROMA OR HALVED GRAPE TOMATOES FOR THEM. YOU MAY ALSO USE 2 CUPS CHOPPED COOKED CHICKEN FOR THE SCALLOPS OR SHRIMP. ADD CHICKEN IN STEP 2.

VEGETARIAN

GO MEATLESS ONCE IN A WHILE. IT'S AN EASY WAY TO GET THE GOOD STUFF YOUR BODY NEEDS. TRY THESE VEGGIECENTRIC RECIPES THAT RELY ON CANNED BEANS, QUICK-COOKING GRAINS, AND PREPREPARED PRODUCE TO KEEP MEALTIME PREP MINIMAL.

BULGUR-CAULIFLOWER BOWLS WITH OLIVE DRESSING

MAKES 4 SERVINGS

2 cups boiling water

1 cup bulgur

2 cups chopped cauliflower or riced cauliflower

½ cup pitted Kalamata and/or green olives, coarsely chopped

3 Tbsp. lemon juice

3 Tbsp. olive oil

1 small clove garlic, minced
Black pepper

4 cups greens, such as escarole, Belgian endive, and/or endive

3 cups thinly sliced celery

1 15-oz. can Great Northern or butter beans, rinsed and drained

1 cup crumbled feta cheese (4 oz.)

1. In a large heatproof bowl pour the boiling water over bulgur. Cover and let stand 15 minutes.

2. Meanwhile, place chopped cauliflower, if using, in a food processor. Cover and pulse three to five times or just until finely chopped.

3. For dressing, in a small bowl combine olives, lemon juice, oil, and garlic. Season to taste with pepper.

4. Drain bulgur; return to large bowl. Stir in cauliflower. Divide mixture among serving bowls. Top with remaining ingredients and serve with dressing.

EACH SERVING 456 cal., 23 g fat (7 g sat. fat), 33 mg chol., 1,185 mg sodium, 49 g carb., 13 g fiber, 4 g sugars, 16 g pro.

[MAKE A SWAP]

THE GREENS SUGGESTED HERE HAVE A SLIGHTLY BITTER FLAVOR. MILD GREENS, SUCH AS SPINACH, BUTTERHEAD, AND BABY KALE, ARE EQUALLY GOOD.

ITALIAN-STYLE FRIED FARRO

HEALTHY	SUPER QUICK	MAKES 4 SERVINGS

2 Tbsp. olive oil

1 10-oz. pkg. shaved Brussels sprouts*

½ cup coarsely chopped red onion

2 oz. thinly sliced prosciutto, cut into thin strips

½ cup chopped walnuts

2 cloves garlic, minced

3 cups cooked farro,** chilled

2 Tbsp. balsamic glaze

2 Tbsp. shredded Parmesan cheese

2 Tbsp. chopped fresh basil
Cracked black pepper

1. In a wok or extra-large nonstick skillet heat 1 Tbsp. of the oil over medium-high. Add Brussels sprouts and onion; cook and stir about 4 minutes or just until crisp-tender. Add prosciutto, walnuts, and garlic; cook and stir 2 minutes. Add farro and the remaining 1 Tbsp. oil. Cook and stir 3 to 4 minutes more or until heated through.

2. To serve, drizzle balsamic glaze over sprouts mixture. Sprinkle with cheese, basil, and pepper.

*Tip If you can't find packaged shaved Brussels sprouts, you can cut 10 oz. fresh Brussels sprouts into thin slices.

**Tip To cook farro, in a medium saucepan combine 3 cups reduced-sodium chicken broth or water and 1¼ cups farro. Bring to boiling; reduce heat. Cover and simmer 25 to 30 minutes or until farro is tender. Drain if necessary.

EACH SERVING 461 cal., 20 g fat (3 g sat. fat), 17 mg chol., 393 mg sodium, 56 g carb., 10 g fiber, 4 g sugars, 17 g pro.

INDIAN-SPICED LENTILS WITH SPINACH

INSTANT MEAL	MAKES 8 SERVINGS

5   cups reduced-sodium chicken or vegetable broth

3   cups uncooked brown lentils, rinsed and drained

1   14.5-oz. can diced tomatoes, undrained

1   cup finely chopped carrots

½   cup chopped onion

2   fresh serrano chile peppers, seeded and finely chopped (tip, page 92)

1   tsp. salt

1   tsp. ground cumin

1   tsp. ground coriander

½   tsp. ground turmeric

1   14-oz. can unsweetened coconut milk

1   5-oz. pkg. baby spinach

    Black pepper

    Hot cooked basmati or brown rice

    Orange wedges

1. In a 6-qt. multifunction electric or stove-top pressure cooker combine the first 10 ingredients (through turmeric). Lock lid in place. Set electric cooker on high pressure to cook 15 minutes. For stove-top cooker, bring up to pressure over medium-high; reduce heat enough to maintain steady (but not excessive) pressure. Cook 15 minutes. Remove from heat. For both models, let stand 15 minutes to release pressure naturally. Release any remaining pressure. Open lid carefully.

2. Stir in coconut milk and spinach. Season to taste with black pepper and additional salt. Serve over rice with orange wedges.

EACH SERVING 484 cal., 9 g fat (8 g sat. fat), 0 mg chol., 823 mg sodium, 78 g carb., 10 g fiber, 5 g sugars, 23 g pro.

CHOPPED SALAD TACOS

HEALTHY	SUPER QUICK	MAKES 4 SERVINGS

2 ears of corn, husks and silks removed

1 15-oz. can pinto beans, rinsed and drained

1 cup chopped zucchini

1 8-oz. container refrigerated guacamole

8 6-inch flour tortillas

½ cup salsa

1. Cut corn kernels from cobs. In a medium bowl combine corn, beans, and zucchini.

2. Spread guacamole on tortillas. Top with vegetable mixture and salsa. Fold in half to serve.

EACH SERVING 440 cal., 16 g fat (3 g sat. fat), 0 mg chol., 1,049 mg sodium, 60 g carb., 9 g fiber, 7 g sugars, 15 g pro.

[SPEED IT UP]

FROZEN WHOLE KERNEL CORN CAN BE USED INSTEAD OF THE FRESH EARS. PLACE 1 CUP CORN IN A COLANDER AND POUR BOILING WATER OVER IT TO THAW. FOR EXTRA FLAVOR, LOOK FOR FROZEN ROASTED CORN.

HOT-AND-SOUR DUMPLING SOUP

HEALTHY	MAKES 6 SERVINGS

4 oz. fresh shiitake mushrooms, stemmed and sliced, or button mushrooms, sliced (1½ cups)

1 Tbsp. vegetable oil

1 32-oz. box reduced-sodium vegetable broth

1 16-oz. pkg. frozen Thai vegetable gyoza dumplings or two 9- to 10-oz. pkg. frozen potstickers

¾ cup shredded carrots

¼ cup rice vinegar or white vinegar

2 Tbsp. reduced-sodium soy sauce

1 tsp. sugar

1 tsp. grated fresh ginger or ¼ tsp. ground ginger

¼ tsp. crushed red pepper

2 green onions, thinly slivered

1. In a large saucepan cook and stir mushrooms in hot oil over medium about 6 minutes or until tender. Add the next eight ingredients (through crushed red pepper). Bring to boiling; reduce heat. Simmer, covered, 2 minutes. Stir in green onions. If soup is too thick, stir in water as needed.

EACH SERVING *162 cal., 4 g fat (1 g sat. fat), 0 mg chol., 654 mg sodium, 28 g carb., 3 g fiber, 9 g sugars, 3 g pro.*

[FINISH WITH FLAVOR]

SQUEEZE SOME SRIRACHA SAUCE OR YOUR FAVORITE ASIAN CHILI SAUCE ON TOP OF THIS SOUP.

GNOCCHI, SWEET CORN, AND ARUGULA IN CREAM SAUCE

MAKES 6 SERVINGS

1 17.6-oz. pkg. shelf-stable potato gnocchi

2 ears of corn or 2 cups frozen whole kernel corn

1 lemon

¾ cup half-and-half

1 5.2-oz. pkg. semisoft cheese with garlic and fines herbes

¼ tsp. black pepper

3 cups torn arugula

Chopped fresh basil (optional)

1. In a 4- to 5-qt. Dutch oven cook gnocchi according to package directions, adding corn the last 5 minutes of cooking. If using ears of corn, transfer ears with tongs to a cutting board. Drain gnocchi, reserving ½ cup of the cooking water. Do not rinse. When fresh corn is cool enough to handle, cut kernels from cobs. Return gnocchi and corn kernels to Dutch oven.

2. For cream sauce, remove 1 tsp. zest and squeeze 1 Tbsp. juice from lemon. In a medium saucepan combine zest and juice, half-and-half, semisoft cheese, and pepper. Cook over medium 10 minutes, stirring frequently. Stir in the reserved ½ cup gnocchi cooking water.

3. Pour cream sauce over gnocchi mixture; heat through. Stir in arugula. If desired, sprinkle with basil.

EACH SERVING 349 cal., 17 g fat (11 g sat. fat), 44 mg chol., 666 mg sodium, 43 g carb., 1 g fiber, 3 g sugars, 8 g pro.

[MAKE A SWAP]

EXPERIMENT WITH DIFFERENT FLAVORS OF SHELF-STABLE OR FROZEN GNOCCHI, SUCH AS SWEET POTATO, SPINACH, AND CAULIFLOWER.

MEDITERRANEAN SALAD ON MINI NAAN

SUPER QUICK	MAKES 4 SERVINGS

3 Tbsp. balsamic vinegar

3 Tbsp. olive oil

1 Tbsp. honey

½ tsp. salt

4 cups baby arugula

1 15-oz. can garbanzo beans (chickpeas), rinsed and drained

1 8-oz. pkg. bite-size fresh mozzarella balls

½ cup pitted Kalamata olives

½ cup torn fresh basil leaves

4 miniature naan or flatbreads

1. For dressing, in a small screw-top jar combine vinegar, olive oil, honey, and salt. Cover and shake well.

2. In a large bowl combine arugula, chickpeas, mozzarella, olives, and basil. Drizzle with dressing; toss to coat. Heat naan according to package directions. Serve arugula mixture over naan.

EACH SERVING 524 cal., 29 g fat (9 g sat. fat), 40 mg chol., 1,368 mg sodium, 42 g carb., 5 g fiber, 9 g sugars, 19 g pro.

GRAIN AND VEGGIE BOWLS

HEALTHY	MAKES 2 SERVINGS

- 2 cups assorted vegetables, such as cherry tomatoes, broccoli or cauliflower florets, shredded carrots, sliced avocado or cucumber, and/or baby spinach
- 1 cup cooked bulgur, quinoa, or farro
- ⅔ cup cooked frozen edamame
- 2 soft-boiled eggs,* peeled and halved
- ¼ cup toasted spiced chickpeas or fried onion salad topper
- ½ cup Romesco Sauce or desired dressing

1. Divide assorted vegetables, bulgur, and edamame between bowls. Top with eggs and chickpeas. Drizzle with Romesco Sauce.

*Tip To make soft-boiled eggs, place eggs in a small saucepan with enough cold water to cover by 1 inch. Bring to boiling over high heat. Remove from heat, cover, and let stand 6 minutes for soft yolk or 8 minutes for jammy yolks; drain. Place in ice water until cool enough to handle; drain.

Romesco Sauce In a food processor combine 1 cup cut-up, seeded roma tomatoes; 1 slice crusty bread (1 oz.), torn; ⅔ cup chopped roasted red sweet pepper; ½ cup blanched almonds; ⅓ cup olive oil; ¼ cup sherry vinegar or red wine vinegar; 2 cloves garlic, chopped; 1 tsp. smoked paprika; and ½ tsp. salt. Cover and process until smooth.

EACH SERVING 518 cal., 30 g fat (4 g sat. fat), 187 mg chol., 417 mg sodium, 44 g carb., 13 g fiber, 7 g sugars, 23 g pro.

ORECCHIETTE WITH RICOTTA AND CHARD PAN SAUCE

MAKES 4 SERVINGS

3 cups dried orecchiette pasta (12 oz.)

1 large bunch green or rainbow Swiss chard

2 Tbsp. olive oil

2 oz. ricotta salata, Asiago, or pecorino cheese, freshly grated

2 Tbsp. butter

Crushed red pepper (optional)

Black pepper and/or grated nutmeg

¼ cup whole milk ricotta cheese

Sea salt

1. Bring a large pot of salted water to boiling. Add orecchiette to boiling water. Cook 10 minutes.

2. Meanwhile, separate chard stems from leaves; cut stems and leave in bite-size pieces. In a large skillet heat olive oil over medium-high. Add chard stems; cook and stir 3 to 5 minutes or until crisp-tender.

3. After pasta has cooked 10 minutes, add chard leaves to pot; cook 2 minutes. Drain, reserving ¼ cup of the cooking liquid. Return pasta and chard to pot. Place over low heat. Add reserved cooking liquid, chard stems, ricotta salata, butter, and, if desired, crushed red pepper, to pasta; toss to combine. Season with pepper and/or nutmeg. Divide pasta mixture among bowls. Top with ricotta. Season with sea salt and additional black pepper and ricotta salata to taste.

EACH SERVING 530 cal., 21 g fat (6 g sat. fat), 42 mg chol., 850 mg sodium, 70 g carb., 4 g fiber, 4 g sugars, 16 g pro.

SPRING MINESTRONE

| HEALTHY | MAKES 4 SERVINGS |

2 Tbsp. olive oil

1 medium leek, thinly sliced

2 cloves garlic, minced

¼ tsp. salt

3 cups reduced-sodium chicken broth

2 cups water

1 bay leaf

1 15- to 16-oz. can Great Northern or cannellini (white kidney) beans, rinsed and drained

8 oz. fresh asparagus spears, trimmed and cut into 2-inch pieces

3 cups coarsely chopped spring greens

4 slices sourdough or French bread

½ cup crumbled aged goat cheese or finely shredded Parmesan cheese (2 oz.)

1. In a large pot heat 1 Tbsp. of the oil over medium. Add leek, garlic, and salt. Cook and stir about 5 minutes or until tender. Stir in broth, the water, and bay leaf; bring to boiling. Stir in beans and asparagus. Return to boiling; reduce heat. Simmer, uncovered, 3 to 4 minutes or until asparagus is tender. Discard bay leaf. Stir in greens.

2. Meanwhile, for cheese toasts, preheat broiler. Brush the remaining 1 Tbsp. oil over both sides of bread slices. Arrange on a baking sheet. Broil 3 to 4 inches from the heat 1 minute per side. Sprinkle with cheese; broil about 1 minute more or until light brown. Serve with soup.

EACH SERVING 292 cal., 12 g fat (4 g sat. fat), 11 mg chol., 996 mg sodium, 33 g carb., 7 g fiber, 4 g sugars, 15 g pro.

FATTOUSH SALAD

HEALTHY	MAKES 4 SERVINGS

2 whole wheat pita bread rounds, torn into bite-size pieces

Nonstick cooking spray

¼ cup olive oil

¼ cup lemon juice

2 cloves garlic, minced

½ tsp. ground sumac (optional)

¼ tsp. kosher salt

¼ tsp. black pepper

4 cups torn romaine lettuce

¾ cup seeded and coarsely chopped cucumber

½ cup sliced radishes

½ cup sliced green onions

¼ cup chopped fresh mint and/or Italian parsley

½ cup crumbled ricotta salata (2 oz.)

4 soft-boiled eggs (tip, page 267), peeled and halved

1. Preheat oven to 350°F. Place pita pieces in a 15×10-inch baking pan and lightly coat with cooking spray. Bake 10 to 15 minutes or until golden and crisp.

2. For dressing, in an extra-large bowl whisk together the next six ingredients (through pepper).

3. Add the next five ingredients (through mint) to bowl; toss to coat. Add pita pieces and cheese; toss to combine. Top with soft-boiled eggs.

EACH SERVING 331 cal., 24 g fat (5 g sat. fat), 13 mg chol., 486 mg sodium, 24 g carb., 3 g fiber, 3 g sugars, 6 g pro.

[MAKE A SWAP]

RICOTTA SALATA CAN BE HARD TO FIND. A GOOD SUBSTITUTE IS FETA CHEESE. FETA HAS A TANGIER FLAVOR, BUT ITS TEXTURE IS SIMILAR TO RICOTTA SALATA.

HURRIED GAZPACHO AND HANDHELD QUESADILLAS

MAKES 4 SERVINGS

2   14- to 16-oz. containers refrigerated fresh salsa

1   cup tomato juice

½   cup fresh cilantro leaves

3   Tbsp. lime juice

2   Tbsp. olive oil

8   6-inch corn tortillas
    Nonstick cooking spray

1   cup shredded taco cheese or Mexican-style four-cheese blend (4 oz.)

½   cup canned black beans, rinsed and drained

½   cup sliced pitted ripe olives

¾   cup plain Greek yogurt or sour cream

1. For gazpacho, in a large bowl stir together salsa, tomato juice, cilantro, lime juice, and oil.

2. For quesadillas, lightly coat both sides of tortillas with cooking spray. Heat an extra-large skillet over medium. Add three of the tortillas; sprinkle half of each tortilla with 2 Tbsp. cheese, 1 Tbsp. beans, and 1 Tbsp. olives. Fold in half; press lightly. Cook 2 minutes; turn and cook 2 to 3 minutes more or until cheese is melted and tortillas are light brown. Remove from skillet. Repeat with remaining tortillas, cheese, beans, and olives.

3. Serve yogurt with gazpacho and quesadillas.

EACH SERVING 440 cal., 22 g fat (8 g sat. fat), 36 mg chol., 1,288 mg sodium, 45 g carb., 5 g fiber, 12 g sugars, 15 g pro.

MUSHROOM AGNOLOTTI WITH CORN, TOMATOES, AND ARUGULA PAN SAUCE

MAKES 4 SERVINGS

2 ears of corn

2 9-oz. pkg. refrigerated wild mushroom-filled agnolotti or ravioli

¾ cup thinly sliced onion

1 clove garlic, thinly sliced

2 Tbsp. olive oil

2 cups chopped tomatoes

2 Tbsp. unsalted butter

1 5-oz. pkg. baby arugula

½ cup finely shredded Parmesan cheese (2 oz.)

1. Cut corn kernels off cobs; set corn aside. In a 4- to 5-qt. Dutch oven bring a large amount of salted water to boiling. Add cobs (to release corn starches and add richness) and agnolotti; cook 6 minutes.

2. Meanwhile, in a large skillet cook onion and garlic in hot oil over medium-high about 2 minutes or until fragrant. Add corn kernels; cook and stir about 1 minute or until crisp-tender. Add tomatoes; cook about 2 minutes more or until tomatoes begin to release some juices, stirring occasionally.

3. Drain pasta, reserving ¼ cup of the cooking water; discard cobs. Return pasta to Dutch oven. Add tomato mixture, reserved pasta cooking water, and the butter; toss gently over low until butter is melted. Add arugula; toss just until wilted. Serve topped with cheese.

EACH SERVING 566 cal., 31 g fat (13 g sat. fat), 102 mg chol., 1,075 mg sodium, 55 g carb., 6 g fiber, 11 g sugars, 23 g pro.

[FINISH WITH FLAVOR]

GIVE THIS DISH SOME FLAIR BY USING MULTICOLOR TOMATOES AND SPRINKLE WITH BIG SHAVINGS OF FRESH PARMESAN CHEESE.

CHEESY GNOCCHI-BROCCOLI SOUP

MAKES 6 SERVINGS

1   14.5-oz. can reduced-
    sodium chicken broth
1   cup chopped peeled
    russet potato
2½ cups milk
1   16-oz. pkg. shelf-stable
    potato gnocchi
2   cups small broccoli florets
1½ cups shredded smoked
    Gouda cheese (6 oz.)
    Black pepper

1. In large saucepan bring broth and potato to boiling; reduce heat. Simmer, covered, 8 minutes. Mash potato slightly. Add milk, gnocchi, and broccoli; bring just to simmering.

2. Gradually add cheese to soup, stirring until it melts. Season to taste with pepper. Serve immediately. If desired, top with additional cheese.

EACH SERVING 322 cal., 10 g fat (6 g sat. fat), 40 mg chol., 687 mg sodium, 42 g carb., 2 g fiber, 7 g sugars, 17 g pro.

VEGETABLE FRIED RICE WITH RED CURRY NUT SAUCE

HEALTHY	MAKES 4 SERVINGS

3 Tbsp. reduced-sodium soy sauce

2 Tbsp. red curry paste

2 Tbsp. cider vinegar

1 Tbsp. peanut butter

¼ tsp. black pepper

1 tsp. canola oil

2 eggs, lightly beaten

2 Tbsp. canola oil

3 cups fresh broccoli florets

1¾ cups fresh julienned or coarsely shredded carrots

1 cup frozen edamame

2 cups cooked white or brown rice, chilled

Dry-roasted peanuts

1. In a small bowl whisk together the first five ingredients (through pepper) until smooth.

2. In an extra-large skillet heat the 1 tsp. canola oil over medium. Add eggs; cook, without stirring, just until set. Stir eggs gently to break into pieces. Remove from skillet.

3. In same skillet heat the 2 Tbsp. canola oil over medium-high. Add broccoli; cook and stir 2 minutes. Reduce heat to medium. Add carrots and edamame; cook and stir 2 to 3 minutes or until crisp-tender. Stir in rice, eggs, and soy mixture; cook 1 to 2 minutes or until heated through. Serve topped with peanuts.

EACH SERVING 354 cal., 17 g fat (2 g sat. fat), 93 mg chol., 701 mg sodium, 37 g carb., 5 g fiber, 6 g sugars, 14 g pro.

[SPEED IT UP]

SAVE TIME PREPPING VEGETABLES. LOOK FOR PACKAGED BROCCOLI FLORETS AND JULIENNED CARROTS IN THE PRODUCE SECTION OF YOUR SUPERMARKET.

MISO-EGG SOUP

HEALTHY	MAKES 4 SERVINGS

4 green onions

1 Tbsp. vegetable oil

6 oz. fresh shiitake mushrooms, stemmed and thinly sliced

1 Tbsp. grated fresh ginger

2 cloves garlic, minced

1 32-oz. carton reduced-sodium chicken or vegetable broth

1 Tbsp. rice vinegar

1 Tbsp. reduced-sodium soy sauce

2 cups baby spinach

⅓ cup white miso paste

⅓ cup hot water

4 eggs

Black pepper

1. Thinly slice green onions, separating white and green parts. In a large deep skillet heat oil over medium. Add white parts of onions, the mushrooms, ginger, and garlic; cook and stir 2 to 3 minutes or until mushrooms begin to soften. Add broth, vinegar, and soy sauce; bring just to boiling.

2. Add spinach. Cook and stir about 30 seconds or until spinach is wilted. In a small bowl combine miso paste and the hot water; stir into broth mixture. Bring just to simmering.

3. Break an egg into a small dish and slip egg into simmering broth. Repeat with remaining eggs. Simmer about 3 minutes or just until yolks are set but still moist, spooning broth over eggs as they cook. Top servings with green parts of onions and sprinkle with black pepper.

EACH SERVING 183 cal., 10 g fat (2 g sat. fat), 186 mg chol., 1,082 mg sodium, 13 g carb., 3 g fiber, 3 g sugars, 12 g pro.

TAHINI-GINGER NOODLES AND VEGGIES

HEALTHY	SUPER QUICK	MAKES 4 SERVINGS

8 oz. dried whole grain linguine

¼ cup tahini (sesame seed paste)

¼ cup lemon juice

¼ cup water

1 Tbsp. grated fresh ginger

1 Tbsp. honey

¼ tsp. kosher salt

2 medium carrots

3 cups broccoli florets

8 oz. sugar snap peas, trimmed and halved diagonally

¼ cup chopped peanuts or almonds

Fresh mint leaves (optional)

1. In a Dutch oven cook linguine in boiling salted water according to pkg. directions; drain. Rinse with cold water; drain again. Return to Dutch oven.

2. Meanwhile, in a small bowl combine the next six ingredients (through salt).

3. Using a vegetable peeler, cut carrots lengthwise into thin ribbons. Add carrots, broccoli, peas, and tahini mixture to linguine; toss to combine. Top with peanuts and, if desired, mint.

EACH SERVING 429 cal., 15 g fat (2 g sat. fat), 0 mg chol., 242 mg sodium, 61 g carb., 9 g fiber, 10 g sugars, 17 g pro.

TOMATOES, GREENS, AND CHICKPEA SKILLET

HEALTHY	MAKES 4 SERVINGS

3 Tbsp. olive oil

½ cup chopped onion

1 clove garlic, minced

1 Tbsp. curry powder

1 15-oz. can garbanzo beans (chickpeas), rinsed and drained

1 14.5-oz. can diced tomatoes, undrained

¼ tsp. salt

2 cups torn Swiss chard or spinach

4 eggs

Salt and black pepper

Fresh cilantro sprigs (optional)

1. In a large skillet heat 2 Tbsp. of the olive oil over medium. Add onion and garlic; cook 5 minutes, stirring occasionally. Add curry powder; cook and stir 1 minute. Add chickpeas, tomatoes, and salt; cook 3 to 4 minutes or until heated through. Add Swiss chard; cook and stir about 3 minutes or until slightly wilted. Remove tomato mixture from skillet; cover to keep warm.

2. Wipe out skillet. Heat the remaining 1 Tbsp. olive oil over medium. Break eggs into skillet; sprinkle with salt and pepper. Cook, covered, until eggs reach desired doneness. Serve tomato mixture with eggs. If desired, top with cilantro.

EACH SERVING 279 cal., 17 g fat (3 g sat. fat), 186 mg chol., 675 mg sodium, 21 g carb., 2 g fiber, 4 g sugars, 12 g pro.

MAC AND FOUR CHEESES

| INSTANT MEAL | MAKES 4 SERVINGS |

2 cups dried elbow macaroni
1 12-oz. can evaporated milk
1 cup water
¼ cup finely chopped onion
½ tsp. garlic powder
¼ tsp. black pepper
⅛ tsp. cayenne pepper
1 cup shredded cheddar cheese (4 oz.)
4 oz. Gruyère or Swiss cheese, shredded (1 cup)
4 oz. smoked Gouda cheese, shredded (1 cup)
¼ cup finely shredded Parmesan cheese (1 oz.)
1 Tbsp. butter
½ cup panko bread crumbs
1 Tbsp. chopped fresh Italian parsley
½ tsp. smoked paprika

1. In a 6-qt. multifunction electric or stove-top pressure cooker stir together the first 11 ingredients (through Parmesan cheese). Lock the lid in place. Set electric cooker on high pressure to cook 3 minutes. For stove-top cooker, bring up to pressure over medium-high heat; reduce heat enough to maintain steady (but not excessive) pressure. Cook 3 minutes. Remove from heat. For both models, let stand 15 minutes to release pressure naturally. Release any remaining pressure. Open lid carefully; stir.

2. Meanwhile, for the crispy topping, in a large skillet melt butter over medium. Add panko; cook and stir about 2 minutes or until golden brown. Remove from heat; stir in parsley and paprika. Sprinkle topping over macaroni mixture.

EACH SERVING 737 cal., 38 g fat (22 g sat. fat), 127 mg chol., 846 mg sodium, 59 g carb., 2 g fiber, 12 g sugars, 38 g pro.

FARRO, BLACK BEAN, AND SPINACH BURRITOS

HEALTHY	INSTANT MEAL	MAKES 8 SERVINGS

1   cup chopped onion

2   cloves garlic, minced

¾   tsp. salt

1   Tbsp. olive oil

1   cup pearled farro, rinsed and drained

1   15-oz. can black beans, rinsed and drained

¾   cup chopped red sweet pepper

3   cups vegetable broth

1   Tbsp. ground coriander

1   tsp. ground cumin

1   cup baby spinach

1   lime

2   cups chopped tomato

1   large ripe avocado, halved, peeled, seeded, and diced

2   green onions, sliced

¼   cup chopped fresh cilantro

8   10-inch flour tortillas, warmed

1   cup shredded Monterey Jack cheese (4 oz.)

1. In a 4- to 6-qt. multifunction electric or stove-top pressure cooker cook onion, garlic, and ¼ tsp. of the salt in hot oil over medium heat until tender. (For electric cooker, use sauté setting.) Stir in the next six ingredients (through cumin).

2. Lock lid in place. Set electric cooker on high pressure to cook 10 minutes. For stove-top cooker, bring up pressure over medium-high heat; reduce heat enough to maintain steady (but not excessive) pressure. Cook 10 minutes. Remove from heat. Let stand 15 minutes to release pressure naturally. Release any remaining pressure. Open lid carefully. Drain if necessary. Stir spinach into farro mixture.

3. For salsa, remove 2 tsp. zest and squeeze 1 Tbsp. juice from lime. In a bowl stir together zest and juice, the remaining ½ tsp. salt, and the next four ingredients (through cilantro). Spoon farro mixture onto warmed tortillas. Top with cheese and salsa. Fold bottom edges of tortillas up and over filling; fold in opposite sides. Roll up tortillas.

EACH SERVING 469 cal., 15 g fat (5 g sat. fat), 13 mg chol., 1,257 mg sodium, 69 g carb., 10 g fiber, 5 g sugars, 17 g pro.

[SPEED IT UP]

START WITH A PURCHASED PICO DE GALLO AND STIR IN CHOPPED AVOCADO RATHER THAN MAKING THE SALSA IN STEP 3.

MUSHROOM AND CHEESE SOURDOUGH TOASTS

MAKES 4 SERVINGS

2 Tbsp. olive oil
1 Tbsp. butter
6 cups sliced assorted fresh mushrooms
2 cloves garlic, minced
1 Tbsp. chopped fresh thyme
   Kosher salt and black pepper
1 tsp. olive oil
4 eggs
4 ½-inch slices rustic sourdough bread
2 cups sliced semisoft cheese, such as Taleggio or Fontina
   Assorted fresh herbs or microgreens

1. Preheat broiler. In a large skillet heat the 2 Tbsp. oil and butter over medium-high. Add mushrooms and garlic; cook about 6 minutes or until mushrooms are tender and brown, stirring occasionally. Remove from heat. Stir in thyme. Season to taste with salt and pepper. Transfer to a bowl.

2. In same skillet heat the 1 tsp. oil over medium. Break eggs into skillet. Reduce heat to medium-low. Cook eggs 3 to 4 minutes or until whites are completely set and yolks begin to thicken.

3. Meanwhile, arrange bread slices on a baking sheet. Broil 4 to 5 inches from heat about 2 minutes or until toasted, turning once. Divide cheese among bread slices; broil about 1 minute more or until cheese is melted and starts to bubble. Top toasts with mushroom mixture, eggs, and assorted herbs.

EACH SERVING 482 cal., 33 g fat (15 g sat. fat), 259 mg chol., 759 mg sodium, 20 g carb., 2 g fiber, 5 g sugars, 28 g pro.

VEGGIE TOSTADAS WITH CAULIFLOWER MASH

MAKES 4 SERVINGS

2 cups cauliflower florets

¼ cup Mexican crema or sour cream

2 Tbsp. coconut oil or olive oil

1 tsp. salt

1 tsp. chopped canned chipotle pepper in adobo sauce

1 cup bite-size pieces fresh asparagus

1 cup frozen whole kernel corn

1 cup quartered grape tomatoes

8 tostada shells

¼ cup crumbled queso blanco or feta cheese (1 oz.)

1. In a covered large saucepan steam cauliflower in a steamer basket over a small amount of boiling water about 4 minutes or until fork-tender. Transfer cauliflower to a food processor. Add Mexican crema, 1 Tbsp. of the oil, ½ tsp. of the salt, and the chipotle pepper. Cover and process until smooth.

2. In covered saucepan steam asparagus and corn in basket over boiling water 4 to 6 minutes or until tender; drain and return to saucepan. Add tomatoes and remaining 1 Tbsp. oil and ½ tsp. salt; toss to coat.

3. Spread tostada shells with cauliflower mixture and top with asparagus mixture. Sprinkle with queso blanco.

EACH SERVING *290 cal., 17 g fat (10 g sat. fat), 15 mg chol., 858 mg sodium, 31 g carb., 5 g fiber, 5 g sugars, 6 g pro.*

[MAKE A SWAP]

FRESH GREEN BEANS COOK IN THE SAME AMOUNT OF TIME AS FRESH ASPARAGUS. TRIM AND CUT AS DIRECTED FOR ASPARAGUS.

SMASHED CHICKPEA SALAD SANDWICHES

HEALTHY	SUPER QUICK	MAKES 4 SERVINGS

1   15-oz. can garbanzo beans (chickpeas), rinsed and drained

½   cup shredded carrot

¼   cup mayonnaise

¼   cup chopped dill pickles

2   tsp. Dijon-style mustard

¼   tsp. dried dill weed

4   small rolls (ciabatta, focaccia wedges, or soft rolls), split

4   slices tomato

1   cup baby kale or spinach

2   thin slices red onion, separated into rings

1. For chickpea salad, in a medium bowl lightly mash chickpeas. Stir in the next five ingredients (through dill weed). Fill rolls with tomato slices, chickpea salad, baby kale, and onion.

EACH SERVING 351 cal., 13 g fat (2 g sat. fat), 6 mg chol., 534 mg sodium, 47 g carb., 6 g fiber, 6 g sugars, 11 g pro.

INDEX

METRIC INFORMATION

PRODUCT DIFFERENCES

Most of the ingredients called for in the recipes in this book are available in most countries. However, some are known by different names. Here are some common American ingredients and their possible counterparts:

SUGAR (white) is granulated, fine granulated, or castor sugar.

POWDERED SUGAR is icing sugar.

ALL-PURPOSE FLOUR is enriched, bleached or unbleached white household flour. When self-rising flour is used in place of all-purpose flour in a recipe that calls for leavening, omit the leavening agent (baking soda or baking powder) and salt.

LIGHT-COLOR CORN SYRUP is golden syrup.

CORNSTARCH is cornflour.

BAKING SODA is bicarbonate of soda.

VANILLA OR VANILLA EXTRACT is vanilla essence.

GREEN, RED, OR YELLOW SWEET PEPPERS are capsicums or bell peppers.

GOLDEN RAISINS are sultanas.

SHORTENING is solid vegetable oil (substitute Copha or lard).

MEASUREMENT ABBREVIATIONS

MEASUREMENT	ABBREVIATIONS
fluid ounce	fl. oz.
gallon	gal.
gram	g
liter	L
milliliter	ml
ounce	oz.
package	pkg.
pint	pt.

COMMON WEIGHT EQUIVALENTS

IMPERIAL / U.S.	METRIC
½ ounce	14.18 g
1 ounce	28.35 g
4 ounces (¼ pound)	113.4 g
8 ounces (½ pound)	226.8 g
16 ounces (1 pound)	453.6 g
1¼ pounds	567 g
1½ pounds	680.4 g
2 pounds	907.2 g

OVEN TEMPERATURE EQUIVALENTS

FAHRENHEIT SETTING	CELSIUS SETTING
300°F	150°C
325°F	160°C
350°F	180°C
375°F	190°C
400°F	200°C
425°F	220°C
450°F	230°C
475°F	240°C
500°F	260°C
Broil	Broil

*For convection or forced air ovens (gas or electric), lower the temperature setting 25°F/10°C when cooking at all heat levels.

APPROXIMATE STANDARD METRIC EQUIVALENTS

MEASUREMENT	OUNCES	METRIC
⅛ tsp.		0.5 ml
¼ tsp.		1 ml
½ tsp.		2.5 ml
1 tsp.		5 ml
1 Tbsp.		15 ml
2 Tbsp.	1 fl. oz.	30 ml
¼ cup	2 fl. oz.	60 ml
⅓ cup	3 fl. oz.	80 ml
½ cup	4 fl. oz.	120 ml
⅔ cup	5 fl. oz.	160 ml
¾ cup	6 fl. oz.	180 ml
1 cup	8 fl. oz.	240 ml
2 cups	16 fl. oz. (1 pt.)	480 ml
1 qt.	64 fl. oz. (2 pt.)	0.95 L

CONVERTING TO METRIC

centimeters to inches	divide centimeters by 2.54
cups to liters	multiply cups by 0.236
cups to milliliters	multiply cups by 236.59
gallons to liters	multiply gallons by 3.785
grams to ounces	divide grams by 28.35
inches to centimeters	multiply inches by 2.54
kilograms to pounds	divide kilograms by 0.454
liters to cups	divide liters by 0.236
liters to gallons	divide liters by 3.785
liters to pints	divide liters by 0.473
liters to quarts	divide liters by 0.946
milliliters to cups	divide milliliters by 236.59
milliliters to fluid ounces	divide milliliters by 29.57
milliliters to tablespoons	divide milliliters by 14.79
milliliters to teaspoons	divide milliliters by 4.93
ounces to grams	multiply ounces by 28.35
ounces to milliliters	multiply ounces by 29.57
pints to liters	multiply pints by 0.473
pounds to kilograms	multiply pounds by 0.454
quarts to liters	multiply quarts by 0.946
tablespoons to milliliters	multiply tablespoons by 14.79
teaspoons to milliliters	multiply teaspoons by 4.93